Unmasking Buddhism

To Adēle

Unmasking Buddhism

Bernard Faure

WILEY-BLACKWELL

A John Wiley & Sons, Ltd., Publication

This edition first published 2009
© 2009 Bernard Faure

Blackwell Publishing was acquired by John Wiley & Sons in February 2007. Blackwell's publishing program has been merged with Wiley's global Scientific, Technical, and Medical business to form Wiley-Blackwell.

Registered Office
John Wiley & Sons Ltd, The Atrium, Southern Gate, Chichester, West Sussex, PO19 8SQ, United Kingdom

Editorial Offices
350 Main Street, Malden, MA 02148-5020, USA
9600 Garsington Road, Oxford, OX4 2DQ, UK
The Atrium, Southern Gate, Chichester, West Sussex, PO19 8SQ, UK

For details of our global editorial offices, for customer services, and for information about how to apply for permission to reuse the copyright material in this book please see our website at www.wiley.com/wiley-blackwell.

The right of Bernard Faure to be identified as the author of this work has been asserted in accordance with the Copyright, Designs and Patents Act 1988.

Library of Congress Cataloging-in-Publication Data

Faure, Bernard.
  Unmasking Buddhism / Bernard Faure.
     p. cm.
  Includes bibliographical references and index.
  ISBN 978-1-4051-8065-8 (hardcover : alk. paper) – ISBN 978-1-4051-8064-1 (pbk. : alk. paper)
1. Buddhism. I. Title.
  BQ4022.F38 2009
  294.3–dc22
                                                 2008049752

A catalogue record for this book is available from the British Library.

Set in 10/12.5pt Meridien
by SPi Publisher Services, Pondicherry, India

1   2009

Contents

Contents

Introduction

The Indian: "What do you want! He has the prejudices of his country, of his party and his own prejudices."

The Japanese: "Oh! See, too many prejudices."

Voltaire, *Philosophical Dictionary*

Unlike Islam, which has suffered a lot of bad press in recent times, Buddhism is seen in a rather more favorable light in Western society today. However, this has not always been the case, as is reflected by Orientalist discourse from the nineteenth century. Western missionaries and colonizers often lumped Islam and Buddhism together and considered them to be the cause of social, economic, political, and spiritual degeneration in the colonized societies. The current high regard in which Buddhism is held is a sign of real progress since that era, when it was met solely with fear or disdain, although this change in attitude remains tinged with ideas of Orientalism.

Today, the media have moved on from their vision of Buddhism as a fashion trend followed by a few intellectuals and now emphasize the sociological importance of this development in Western

1

countries. Despite this trend reversal, what do we actually know about Buddhism? While our knowledge has certainly progressed considerably since the nineteenth century, it is nevertheless often constrained by certain ingrained ideas which restrict the range of issues addressed and questions asked.

The average person on the street is often confronted with certain very specific forms of Buddhism which are presented as if they represent the norm. These include, most notably, Tibetan Buddhism, Zen Buddhism, and Theravāda (or the "Way of the Elders"). Tibetan Buddhism, while strongly influenced by the Indian tradition of the "Great Vehicle" (Mahāyāna), is the result of a specific development, a mixture of Tantrism and scholasticism. The Zen tradition, which appeared during the sixth century in China (under the name of Chan), assumed its current form in medieval Japan. Despite its significance, Zen is merely a branch of the "Great Vehicle" such as it developed principally in China and Japan. The other schools of East Asian Mahāyāna are virtually unheard of in Europe and the United States. Theravāda has become the most dominant form of Buddhism in Sri Lanka and Southeast Asia (Myanmar, Thailand, Cambodia, Laos) and is simply a modernized version of one of the many schools of ancient Buddhism; indeed, it is the only one to have survived.

Despite all of these different forms, for most Westerners the word "Buddhism" evokes primarily Tibetan Buddhism. This version of Buddhism, which is very specific despite making universal claims, is featured on every page of successful books such as *The Monk and the Philosopher*, which features a dialogue between the "philosopher" Jean-François Revel and his son, the "monk" Matthieu Ricard, a disciple of the Dalai Lama. The book provides a handy catalogue of received ideas, which are accurate to a greater or lesser extent, yet also reflects a certain level of orthodoxy that should be examined closely, even if it means playing devil's advocate (or rather Māra's advocate, the Buddhist equivalent). Let's start by exploring some landmarks in time.

Before questioning received ideas about Buddhism, it should be remembered that they often include a significant dose of truth. Furthermore, when these ideas are held by a great many people, they end up becoming truth or at least orthodoxy (literally meaning correct opinion). In Buddhism, these ideas form part of what is known as the conventional truth – as opposed to the ultimate truth. This notion of Two Truths, conventional and ultimate, favors the latter, yet this does not detract from the value of the received opinion: a half-truth still has some truth-claim. Even if they do not go far enough, half-truths are a means of accessing the ultimate truth.

When it comes to the question of who can speak in the name of Buddhism, it is tempting to reply that, obviously, Buddhists can. However, it is less easy to determine who, in fact, Buddhists are. In the absence of criteria accepted by all, it could be said that a Buddhist is someone who declares himself or herself to be one.

While historians and sociologists usually refrain from adopting a stance on the content of the Buddhist doctrine, they are heavily involved in describing the development of this doctrine and the communities that profess to follow it as objectively as possible. From their point of view, there is no Buddhism; strictly speaking, there are only Buddhists. Or, put another way, Buddhism is not an essence in itself, it is something Buddhists do.

However, we quickly come across another stumbling block: in the US, for example, the beliefs and practices of recent – and usually Caucasian – converts differ greatly from those of Buddhists of Asian origins. When one Buddhist declares something in the name of Buddhism and another Buddhist declares the exact opposite, who are we to believe? In this case, historians restrict themselves to analyzing the many available sources and practices with the aim of including rather than excluding.

Sometimes, received ideas about Buddhism are not supported by tradition. These ideas often imply and reinforce each other. The majority are derived from a fundamental bias, which is also an act of faith: the belief in a "pure" Buddhism, devoid of any "superstition," which was miraculously transmitted through various cultures over the centuries to reach the modern Western world. In fact, this Buddhism is a relatively recent invention, the result of a series of reforms in various Asian countries and of increased contact with the West. It has developed in response to colonization, the requirement to modernize, and the influence of Protestantism.

In one sense, these ideas adopted and retained by Buddhists as part of their tradition are part of the Buddhist experience. They also enable us to adopt an initial approach that can be modified as we explore the practices further and develop our understanding – we have to start somewhere after all.

Some of these ideas are simply incorrect while the majority are partially correct but have been overly simplified, thus weakening the Buddhist tradition. They tend to take what was essentially one of many aspects of the doctrine and regard it as a dogma and impose orthodoxy by falsely assuming that certain ideas form part of the long-standing Buddhist tradition. By calling such ideas into question, the complexity and richness of the Buddhist tradition can perhaps be restored, at least in part.

Part I
Buddhism in History

— "Buddhism is both one and many" —

Many received ideas about Buddhism stem from a refusal to take the diversity of Buddhism as a living tradition seriously. Of course, all books which seek to popularize the subject are careful to state that Buddhism is both "one and many," but they nevertheless go on to reduce this multiplicity to one fundamental unity by concentrating on so-called "primitive Buddhism." Some such books jump directly from this "pure" Buddhism, i.e., that of the Buddha himself (as we imagine him), to Tibetan Buddhism, Zen, and Theravāda as if they are all directly derived from this original form. Unable to do justice to the rich diversity of Buddhisms which have evolved through the influence of the various host cultures, they focus upon a few of the simple ideas to which Buddhists of all denominations are supposed to adhere.

The Buddhist doctrine first developed in northern India towards the fifth century BCE and gradually spread its way across the rest of the subcontinent during the third century BCE following the conversion of King Ashoka, founder of the first Indian empire. During the same period, a schism occurred between the disciples of the Buddha that eventually led to a separation into the two main schools – the "Great Vehicle" (Mahāyāna) and the "Lesser Vehicle" (Hīnayāna). The name "Lesser Vehicle" was given to the more conservative of the schools by its critics and rivals of the "Great Vehicle." It later became Theravāda. The distinction between these two "vehicles" is not always as rigid as we are led to believe. Some also distinguish a third school of Buddhism, known as the "Diamond Vehicle" (Vajrayāna), which is also referred to as or esoteric Buddhism or Tantrism (after the name of its canonic texts, the Tantras).

Without King Ashoka, Buddhism may well have remained a minority religion rather like Jainism, with which it shares certain common features. Legend has it that Ashoka ordered the construction

7

of 84,000 *stūpas* throughout India – and indeed beyond, given that some have been found in China – where relics of the Buddha could be deposited. Whatever the case, this model of the Buddhist sovereign embodied by Ashoka had a lasting influence upon the relationship between Buddhism and the state in all Asian cultures. The spread of Buddhism in India led to a proliferation of schools (or "groups," the *nikāya*), which is the reason why this form of early Buddhism is sometimes known as Nikāya Buddhism. However, this expression restricts Buddhism to doctrinal aspects and in doing so fails to take account of the popular religion which does not always stem directly from Nikāya Buddhism.

The factors that contributed to the diversification of Buddhism in India in the centuries following the Buddha's death include the settling of the monks and the great distances between the centers of Buddhism. As the wealth of the monasteries grew, monks and nuns were able to live a more comfortable existence. Their tendency to specialize often led to a polarization between the ascetics, who practiced their religion in the relative solitude of the forests and the village, and city-based monks, who devoted their time to teaching or studying in the great monasteries. These different approaches to doctrine, ritual, and discipline became ever more established with each new religious council.

It was on the occasion of the third council that the first schism occurred between the group of the "Elders" (Pāli: Thera, Sanskrit: Sthavira), partisans of a strict interpretation of the Buddha's teachings, and the majority – the so-called "Great Assembly" (Mahāsānghika) – which tried to adapt this teaching by relying on its spirit rather than on its letter. This schism paved the way to a new form of Buddhism, which named itself Mahāyāna, as opposed to the earlier form of Buddhism which, as we have seen, was referred to as Hīnayāna. The term "vehicle" here means "a way of going towards salvation."

The origin of Mahāyāna Buddhism continues to be the subject of much debate. Some have claimed that it stems from the lay-people reacting against the elitism of the monks and the opulence of the monasteries. Others point to the emergence of new forms of religious practice such as the worshiping of *stūpas* and relics, the worship of Scriptures, and, more generally, devotion to the Buddha. Some scholars have described Mahāyāna as a "fringe sectarian movement" trying to gain economic support. In fact, Mahāyāna seems to be an essentially monastic phenomenon and somewhat militant in nature. It could even be described as military in certain cases, if we are to believe the *Mahāparinirvāna Sutra*: "If a layperson observes the five precepts but does not bear arms to protect the monks, he does not deserve to go by the name of mahāyānist."

Despite its polemic declarations, Mahāyāna complemented rather than excluded Hīnayāna: it considers salvation to be accessible to all, for example, and is more broadly accessible than Hīnayāna – which advocates the strict observance of an ascetic lifestyle.

While the reform of Mahāyāna may have introduced certain lax attitudes, it also developed the more ascetic tendencies of Buddhism, focusing on virtues such as compassion, wisdom, and the use of skillful means (*upāya*) to salvation. On a soteriological level, Awakening (*bodhi*) overrode the previous ideal of *nirvāna*. Where the conception of the Buddha was concerned, relative historicism was transformed into radical docetism and the Buddha, who had become purely "metaphysical," was multiplied. The Buddha's human form was now little more than a white lie intended to gradually guide people towards the truth. On a practical level, the emphasis was placed upon devotion to various buddhas (Amitābha, Akshobhya, Baishajyaguru, Mahāvairochana) and bodhisattvas (Avalokiteshvara, Mañjushrī, Samantabhadra) as well as upon penitence and the transfer of merits.

Mahāyāna thought really took off with the tradition of the Perfection of Wisdom (*prajñāpāramitā*), as expressed in the sutras of the same name. The first of these texts dates from the beginning of the Common Era. They vary in length from one extreme (100,000 verses) to another (the *Hridaya* [*Heart*] *Sutra*) of around one page.

Mahāyāna began to spread throughout central Asia and China around the start of the Common Era and then spread subsequently throughout Korea, Japan, and Vietnam. Hīnayāna (a term we are using here for want of a better one and which we do not intend to have any pejorative connotations whatsoever) was initially transmitted to Sri Lanka during the reign of Ashoka and then, from the tenth century CE, spread throughout Southeast Asia (Myanmar, Thailand, Laos, Cambodia). It lives on today in the form of Theravāda, which has become the dominant form of Buddhism in the countries cited above.

Between the fifth and the seventh centuries CE, a third movement, known as Tantric or esoteric Buddhism, arose. For some scholars, it is a radically new form of Buddhism, a new "Vehicle," known as the "Diamond Vehicle" (Vajrayāna), but in fact it simply adopts many Mahāyāna conceptions, while taking them to their extreme. As in Mahāyāna, the identity between *nirvāna* and *samsāra* (the cycle of life and death) constitutes the basis for Tantric doctrine and practice. Based on this notion, all verbal, physical, and mental acts become acts of the primordial Buddha. Tantric rituals place a great deal of emphasis on symbols of all kinds: invocations (mantra, *dharānī*), hand gestures (*mudrā*) and geometric drawings (*mandala*). This predominance of ritual is one of the features that distinguishes Tantric Buddhism most clearly from previous forms of Buddhism.

This trend spread outside India during the eighth to ninth centuries in Tibet, China, and Japan, as well as in Southeast Asia (Indonesia, Myanmar, Cambodia). It failed to survive in the latter countries but was predominant in Tibet and Japan for many centuries. Even today, it remains the official religion of the small Himalayan state of Bhutan. While it has been heavily indebted to Indian Mahāyāna tradition, Tibetan Buddhism is the result of a specific development, a mix of Tantrism and scholasticism.

Theravāda, the dominant form in Sri Lanka and Southeast Asia, is a modern form of Hīnayāna or Nikāya Buddhism. While it is clearly more conservative than Mahāyāna, it has also considerably evolved in the course of centuries, and cannot be considered to be more representative of "authentic" or "primitive" Buddhism. This tradition developed in Sri Lanka between the third century BCE and the fifth century CE. From here, it spread to Myanmar in the tenth century and then to Thailand and other Indianized states of the Indo-China peninsula (with the exception of Vietnam, which was influenced by Chinese culture) between the thirteenth and fourteenth centuries.

Theravāda therefore served as a culture and religion common to the Indianized countries of Asia, in large part owing to the use of Pāli as a lingua franca. In all of these countries, the "historic" Buddha formed the main object of worship, although this worship was often closely interlinked with other local forms of worship. It should not be forgotten that Theravāda has not always been as "pure" and free from mystical and esoteric elements as we are often led to believe. There was, and still is, a "tantric Theravāda" that is strongly influenced by esoteric speculation.

Thus, in spite of all the talk about "pure" Buddhism, it is clear that Buddhism has constantly evolved, influenced as it was by the eras, places, and cultures which adopted it. It is both anchored in history through its secular roots and living in the world around us today.

—— "The Buddha is only a man who —— achieved Awakening"

In India, the Buddha is a historical person.
Hegel, *Lectures on the Philosophy of Religion*, 1827

Without the "historical" Buddha, Buddhism wouldn't exist. This may seem like stating the obvious, but is it really? If the Buddha hadn't existed, perhaps he would have been invented anyway. This is undoubtedly what happened, regardless of whether or not he did actually exist. In any case, the historicity of the Buddha is hardly ever questioned today, even though we continue to question the historical basis of various events that happened during his long lifetime.

It is certainly easy to accept the notion that the legend of the Buddha is simply derived from an embellished image of a historical person. Pāli texts in particular seem to be based on certain historical facts and the Vinaya monastic codes contain clear attempts to present Buddha as an eminently pragmatic individual. Supporters of this historicist interpretation rightly stress that it is easier to "mythologize" a biography than to "demythologize" a legend.

So what do we actually know about the Buddha? It is fair to say that he was born, he lived, and he died. The rest remains lost in the mists of myth and legend: his immaculate conception his miraculous birth, and so on. The fact that some of these elements are also said to have occurred during the life of the founder of Jainism, Mahāvīra (another allegedly "historical" character), indicates that a degree of caution must be exercised.

Historians have focused on the circumstances surrounding the death of the Buddha in particular. They emphasize one detail which they claim could not have been invented: he is said to have died as a result of eating contaminated pork. It is nothing short of a scandal that such a pre-eminent figure should have spent his last moments crippled by terrible diarrhea as a result of eating meat. Buddhists, now proud of their vegetarianism, have subsequently been keen to reinterpret this tale by swapping the pork for a vegetarian dish. Historians, on the other hand, have sought to establish some kind of historical anchor point for the story and have argued, with a certain degree of sense, that this tale does not seem to be the result of hagiography – which usually seeks to embellish the life of saints.

Siddharta Gautama, the future Buddha, is said to have been born during the fifth century BCE as the son of a king of northern India. His conception and birth were allegedly immaculate. His mother, Queen Māya, dreamt that a white elephant pierced the side of her body; the next morning, she found herself to be pregnant. Nine months later, she gave birth to a child in a grove in Lumbini. The child immediately began to sing a "song of victory," declaring "I alone am the honored one above earth and under heaven." To prove this, he took seven steps in each of the four directions, a lotus flower blossoming with each step he took.

The auspicious nature of the Buddha's birth seems to be contradicted by the death of his mother, seven days later. The orphan was then raised by his aunt, Mahāprajāpati. Following predictions that he would become either a universal monarch or a universal spiritual guide, his father decided to lock him away in the palace to protect him against harsh realities, thereby preventing him from any kind of spiritual pursuit.

At the age of 16, Prince Siddharta married Yashodharā and they had a child, Rāhula (the name means "Obstacle" and speaks volumes about Siddharta's paternal feelings). Other sources claim that he had three spouses overall and followed a traditional career path as monarch. At any rate, destiny had other plans for him in the form of four encounters that took place during an excursion outside of the palace: he met an elderly man, a sick man, a corpse, and an ascetic. The first three encounters made him aware of the transitory nature of existence, while the fourth brought him a sense of deliverance. As a result, at the age of 29, Siddharta fled from the palace and abandoned his princely duties and prerogatives. For six years, he practiced all kinds of austerities which almost got the better of him. Having finally realized the futility of these practices, he discovered the "Middle Way" – a path between hedonistic pleasure and asceticism – and came up against the Buddhist Devil, Māra, and his enticing daughters. Having successfully resisted this temptation, there was nothing more to block his path to Awakening. During this ultimate stage, he gradually passed through the four stages of meditation (*dhyāna*), became aware of his previous lives, and eventually realized the "Four Noble Truths."

This story of the Buddha's life, culminating in Awakening and the final *nirvāna*, is first and foremost a digest of doctrine and a paradigm of Buddhist practice. When it comes to Enlightenment (or Awakening), through which the Buddha is able to transcend his physical self, it is this same life – the same psychodrama or cosmodrama of Awakening – that is repeated in all past and future buddhas. This explains the extreme monotony of these lives, all based on the same model. The same can be said, in part, of the lives of the saints, which are also "imitations" of the life of the Buddha. All are said to have passed through the same stages as the Buddha: a spiritual crisis followed by a renouncement of the world, an ascetic existence leading to Awakening, the acquisition of extraordinary powers, preaching and gathering disciples, jealousy caused by success and criticism of a corrupt society, death foretold, and a funeral that gives rise to the worship of relics.

Interestingly, the life of the Buddha also had an influence upon the lives of the Christian saints. The main aspects of the Buddha's life were known to the West from an early point in time. They gradually infiltrated the medieval imagination through the "golden legend" of Christianity which was itself influenced by Arabic legend. This is reflected for instance in the story of Barlaam and Josaphat. The latter (whose name appears to be an adaptation of "bodhisattva") was the son of an Indian king who persecuted the Christians, and he lived alone in his father's palace until one day he encountered a leper, a blind man, and an elderly man. These meetings enabled him to realize the evanescent nature of existence and he was then converted to Christianity by an ascetic named Barlaam. This conversion led to martyrdom (which does not feature in the original Buddhist version of events).

Early Buddhism centered around the worship of *stūpas*, memorials which focus on the main episodes of this unusual "life" – in particular the four *stūpas* which commemorate Buddha's birth, Awakening, first sermon, and final *nirvāna* which went on to become much-visited sites of pilgrimage. As a result, the life of the Buddha took a monumental turn, in every sense of the word.

By visiting these sites, followers were able to relive each and every glorious episode of the life of their master and fill their imagination with these places. However, these *stūpas* were more than just simple commemorative monuments; they were also primarily mausoleums or reliquaries containing parts of the body of Buddha. Contact with or proximity to these relics was said to have magical efficacy increasing the chances of happiness in this world and of salvation in the other world. One of these builders of *stūpas* went on to have a massive impact upon the development of the Buddhist religion. This person was King Ashoka, whose empire extended right across India. Ashoka went on a pilgrimage to the birthplace of the Buddha in Lumbini, where he erected a commemorative pillar. However, tradition has it that he also ordered the construction of 80,000 *stūpas* where relics of Buddha would be deposited. His role as a Buddhist sovereign played a significant role in the relationship between Buddhism and sovereignty in all the cultures of Asia. Without Ashoka, Buddhism would most likely have remained a minority religion, like Jainism, with which it shares certain common features. The history of early Buddhism is essentially one of a community of followers and pilgrims and this legend and its constant developments have had a far greater influence upon its rapid expansion than the actual "historical" individual – the Buddha himself.

Having increased the number of episodes relating to the life of the Buddha, legend then turned to the Buddha's past lives. According to the Buddhist doctrine of karma, the Buddha's present life was simply the result of a long series of previous lives which saw the Bodhisattva reincarnated as various different beings, both animals and humans. These past lives form the focus of texts known as *Jātakas*. This same model is applied to the existence of other past buddhas. There is also mention of the future buddha, Maitreya, who it is said will appear in several millions of years, although his "biography" remains somewhat vague. The Mahāyāna tradition in particular speaks of numerous metaphysical buddhas which are already present – although invisible to the human eye.

Initially presented as some kind of superhuman being, the Buddha is therefore gradually transformed into a god. Some of the Mahāyāna texts document this development. In the Lotus sutra, for instance, the Buddha himself calls his own historical authenticity into question. This coup de théâtre takes place in a text with wide-ranging influence across Asia. During a sermon, the Buddha declares to his disciples that he has already guided numerous beings towards salvation. Faced with their skepticism, he calls upon these beings to show themselves, and a multitude of bodhisattvas ("Awakened beings") suddenly spring up from the ground. While his disciples wonder how he has been able to carry out this task during his existence as a human, he reveals that his life is, in fact, eternal. He states that he employed "skillful means," claiming to have been born in the form of Prince Siddharta, to have left his family, and to have spent six years of austerity to finally achieve Awakening – to convince those of weak capacity. He states that the time has come to reveal the truth of the situation, namely that he has essentially always been the Awakened One. The weak-spirited (which refers to the followers of Hīnayāna) will, he says, continue to believe in the conventional truth of the biography of the Buddha, whereas his most advanced disciples will know the ultimate truth – the transcendent nature of the Buddha.

So where does the belief in a "historical" Buddha come from? What does this belief signify and how can it be reconciled with the proliferation of "metaphysical" buddhas associated with the Mahāyāna tradition? Westerners (as well as certain "Westernized" Asians) first developed a firm belief in the historical authenticity of the Buddha during the nineteenth century at a time when triumphant rationalism was seeking an alternative to Christianity. The Orientalist scholars who discovered Buddhism wanted to see it as a religion which would tie in with their own views: rather than being a religion revealed by a transcendent God, this was seen to be a human, moral, and rational religion founded by an extremely wise individual. According to Michel-Jean-François Ozeray, author of a book entitled *Recherches sur Buddou ou Bouddhou, instituteur religieux de l'Asie Orientale* (1817): "Descended from the altar where he was placed through blind faith and superstition, Buddou is a distinguished philosopher, a sage born for the happiness of his fellow men and the goodness of humanity." The Buddha, remodeled to suit the cause, was henceforth considered to be a freethinker who opposed the superstitions and prejudices of his time.

Attempts were then made to apply to the "biography" of the Buddha the same methods of critical historical analysis applied to Christ (a process which continues even today). As a result, the "historical" Buddha began to overshadow all the "metaphysical" buddhas of the Mahāyāna tradition, thus relegating this tradition to the realms of fantasy while Theravāda, which is said to be alone in preserving the memory of its founder, found itself promoted to the rank of "authentic" Buddhism.

My purpose here is not to deny the authenticity of a man who once went by the name of the Buddha, but instead to highlight the fact that the question itself is irrelevant, except for a historicist – that is, Western – approach. The question is certainly of little consequence for traditional Buddhists, who see the life of the Buddha, above all, as a model and an ideal to be followed. The "imitation" of this timeless paradigm is a fundamental fact of monastic life. It is not just about achieving Awakening for oneself by identifying with the Buddha individually; it also involves re-creating the Buddhist community utopia of the early days: bringing the Buddha back to life not just as a detached individual, but rather in close symbiosis with his disciples.

So why is establishing the historical authenticity of the Buddha of such great importance to us? Because the authenticity of the life of the "founder" is the only guarantee of the originality of the religion he founded. Without a concrete biography, the Buddha disappears into the mists of time, and without the

Buddha, Buddhism itself seems to become dangerously plural. Indeed, what does the conservative and somewhat puritanical Hīnayāna (nowadays represented by Theravāda) Buddhism have in common with the abundance of images and mystical fervor of Mahāyāna Buddhism – and more specifically Tantric Buddhism, which is based on magic, sexuality, and transgression? In fact these two movements, while initially opposed, ended up complementing one another. While a religion based on orthodoxy (such as the monotheisms of the West) would have anathemized heresy, Buddhism embraces more or less all of these competing or apparently irreconcilable trends. In this sense, it is perhaps preferable to talk of a Buddhist nebula rather than a unified religion. The image of the Buddha, which is constantly being renewed, is one of the elements that have enabled Buddhists of all denominations to identify with the same tradition. In this sense, the "historical" Buddha is simply another work of fiction, the most recent in a long line of tradition marked by constant reinventions of the image of the Buddha.

—— "Buddhism is an Indian religion" ——

In 1935, the French scholar Paul Mus said of Buddhism that "India produced it, India will explain it." Similarly, according to art historian Alfred Foucher, "As with all products of the Indian genius, Buddhism, for us, is both intelligible and inadmissible, near and far, similar and disparate." (*Étude sur l'iconographie bouddhique de l'Inde*, 1900–5). Nevertheless, focusing solely on the Indian origins of the religion underestimates the fundamental contribution made by other Asian societies (of Tibet, China, Korea, and Japan, to name just the main ones) to the development of Buddhism. Paul Mus himself was well aware of the significance of local influences on the Buddhism of Southeast Asia, a subject which he wrote about at length.

What is striking, however, when one reads books about "Indian" Buddhism, is the extent to which it is discussed outside of its particular cultural context. To be sure, Buddhist legend makes reference to various more or less historical events. We are also told that the Buddha rejected both the Indian caste system and brahmanic sacrifice. Western works on Buddhism rarely refer to the other great Indian religious movements (Jainism, Shivaism, Vishnuism). In these accounts, Buddhism is often presented as simply existing independently of Hinduism rather than contradicting it. You could almost believe that the first Buddhist monks lived on a different planet to the followers of other Indian religions, whereas they in fact came into contact with one another on a daily basis.

Western researchers quickly sought to establish a contrast between Buddhism, with its path to salvation open to all individuals making it essentially "universal," and other religious movements of the day which were considered to be typically Indian and as such too embedded in local culture. They give the impression that Buddhism is first and foremost a reaction against Hinduism, a rejection of purely Indian values and an attempt at dispensing with any cultural or social conditioning. As a result, the Buddha is paradoxically presented as a thinker whose ideas strangely resemble those of a rationalist mind at the end of the nineteenth century.

At the other extreme, certain Indian publications on Buddhism focus on its Indian roots, and enroll the new religion in the cause of Indian nationalism. Historians researching Buddhism, while they have avoided these extremes, have nevertheless often presented Indian Buddhism as the Buddhism par excellence due to their innate tendency to trace everything back to its origins, the result being that other historical forms of the tradition (Chinese and Japanese Buddhism, for instance) have been depicted as mere by-products. There are a few notable exceptions to this: Theravāda, which allegedly preserved the purity of "primitive" Buddhism; Tibetan Buddhism, which can claim an eminent spiritual filiation owing to the Dalai Lamas; and Japanese Zen, which claims to be the essence of the Buddha's Awakening.

We are also often told that Indian Buddhism was a reform of Hinduism (or Brahmanism) – by which one means essentially that the Buddha reformed the caste system. But social reform is quickly identified with religious reform, leading to the claim that Buddhism was to Hinduism "rather like the Reformation in Europe was to Catholicism" (*Le Globe*, 25 November 1829). As a result, we forget all too quickly that the earliest form of Buddhism was, in principle, a new Indian religion: to make a valid comparison, you would have to compare the relationship between Buddhism and Hinduism to the relationship between Christianity and Judaism, or even Islam and Christianity.

Given the prestige accorded to its origins, it is surprising that Western Buddhists tend to favor Tibetan Buddhism. One of two things must be true: either the "true doctrine" of Buddhism is that of the Buddha and his closest disciples, making Tibetan Buddhism a distant and somewhat suspect derivative (with its Tantric rituals and imagery, and its theory of successive reincarnation), or else the orthodox form has developed and been enriched over the centuries, which would make Tibetan Buddhism only one of various possible scenarios to arise from this supple and multiple orthodoxy. The same reasoning applies to Theravāda, which despite its claims has come a long way from the "original" teachings of the Buddha.

Every time it has come into contact with a different Asian culture, Buddhism has undergone a unique evolution and adapted; while some of these adaptations may seem more interesting or attractive to us in the West than others, this does not mean that they are spiritually superior in any way. Whatever the case, it is essential to address all forms of Buddhism without adopting any attitude of sectarianism and without echoing national prejudices.

The most striking thing about current research in the field is the near-imperviousness of the various disciplines. With a few notable exceptions, scholars of Indian culture have mostly ignored Buddhism while so-called Buddhologists have similarly chosen to overlook non-Buddhist India. These same specialists have also tended to disregard or devalue other forms of Buddhism, notably those of East Asia. However, these forms of Buddhism have no reason to envy Theravāda or Tibetan Buddhism in terms of doctrine of practice.

Just as it is said that Rome is no longer in Rome, it could also be said that India is no longer merely in India. It can be found at the extreme tip of Europe through Indo-European ideology as well as at the extreme tip of Asia in medieval Japan through the expansion of Buddhism. Georges Dumézil deserves a mention here. His work, more than any other, has made it possible to understand the extent to which ideological constructions of India have influenced the cultures of the Indo-European sphere. These ideas can still be found, sometimes virtually unchanged, as far away as the shores of the Atlantic and Baltic.

Somewhat paradoxically, Buddhism as we perceive it today is both too Indian and not Indian enough. It is too Indian in the sense that Indian Buddhism has come to be regarded as representing "classic" Buddhism, to the detriment of other equally significant forms of Buddhism. The importance of the Tibetan and Sino-Japanese canons relative to the Pāli and Sanskrit canons is often underestimated, in terms of both their volume and their doctrinal content. It is not Indian enough in the sense that this "classic" Buddhism has become a kind of "vacuum-packed" Buddhism, independent of its cultural and social background. Real-life Buddhism, Indian or otherwise, is a different story – a story which has still to be written and which will be very different.

Let's pause a moment to consider this emphasis on Indian Buddhism – which is at first glance justified given the cultural significance it holds in both Asia and the West. On a specifically philosophical level, however, the primacy of Indian Buddhism is less justifiable, especially in relation to Jainism, another far-reaching religious, cultural, and philosophical system. Yet does

21

our knowledge about the Jainist movement, which appears to have been founded by a contemporary of the Buddha, extend beyond a few vague clichés?

Furthermore, one Buddhism can conceal another. Interest in "classic Buddhism" – and its two forms known as the Great and Lesser Vehicles – has taken the spotlight away from other philosophical and religious movements such as Tantric Buddhism – which is often relegated to the ranks of magic or superstition. We need to move away from the notion that philosophical reflection peaked in Buddhism with the Indian Mādhyamika ("Middle Way") tradition and that the remainder are merely footnotes on Nāgārjuna's *Fundamental Verses on the Middle Way*.

Paradoxically, talking about the Western lack of awareness of India – as does Roger-Pol Droit in his stimulating book entitled *L'Oubli de l'Inde* – equates to discussing the West rather than India. Similarly, talking about Buddhist philosophy equates to discussing philosophy rather than Buddhism.

If we consider the Buddhist tradition in terms of its geographical expansion and the spread of its doctrine, and not just in terms of its ideal proximity to Indian sources, it becomes evident that it has suffered serious prejudice at the hands of historians. As mentioned previously, Buddhism emerged in the north of India around the fifth century BCE and spread throughout Asia over the course of the following ten centuries. With the exception of Zen, the Sino-Japanese Buddhist tradition had been strangely overlooked until recently by both Sinologists and Buddhologists alike.

Just as Western thought is based on Greco-Roman and Judeo-Christian ideas, Buddhist thought has been able to assimilate two cultures as radically different as those of India and China, not to mention Indianized and Sinicized, yet original, cultures such as those of Tibet and Japan. In order to understand Buddhist thought and the ways in which it has been complicated and revived by local religions, we need to move away from India and take into account Asia as a whole.

While developing the potential of Mahāyāna, Chinese Buddhism has opened up to the influence of various non-Buddhist trends, most notably Taoism and Confucianism. It is time to reevaluate the Chinese contribution to Buddhist thought, and notably the considerable philosophical contribution made by the various schools of Chinese Buddhism. By "forgetting" Chinese Buddhism as it did, "Buddhology" and Sinology have become heirs to a Chinese tradition (essentially Confucian) which considers this doctrine to be a "barbaric" religion. The influence of this conception can be found for instance in the works of Victor Segalen, who refers to the "Buddhist heresy" and its detrimental influence upon the China of the Wei dynasty. He even suggests that Buddhism in China is a disease of Chinese thought and Buddhist art in China a disease of Chinese Forms.

India alone is therefore no longer sufficient to explain Buddhism, even though it can explain *Indian* Buddhism – and even though other forms of Buddhism would be incomprehensible without India.

"Buddhism is the cult of nothingness"

Buddhism is a cult of nothingness.
What a thing to worship! We'd say.
Yes, undoubtedly, it's a strange but established fact.

Victor Cousin, 1841

Up until the start of the last century, Buddhism was regarded as a nihilistic doctrine. The idea stemmed from an incorrect interpretation of the notion of *nirvāna* and was upheld, in one form or another, by virtually everyone who wrote on the subject of Buddhism during the nineteenth and at the beginning of the twentieth century. The Catholic writer Paul Claudel, for example,

23

stated, in *Knowing the East*: "The Buddha found only nothingness and his doctrine taught a monstrous communion."

Discussion surrounding "Buddhist nihilism" in the nineteenth century reveals a dark side to European philosophical discourse, causing us to question our current interpretation of Buddhism. A negative Orientalism, which tended to demonize the Buddha, was replaced at the start of the last century by a positive Orientalism with a tendency to idealize Buddhism, without it really being clear how or why. However, it has become increasingly evident that Buddhism is not – and probably never was – the harmonious doctrine its advocates would have us believe.

It is now generally thought that "Buddhism" is a fairly recent construction, dating from the start of the nineteenth century. It was during this era that the neologism first began to appear in texts. However, the predominant impression of Buddhism held today – that of a therapeutic, rational, compassionate, and tolerant doctrine – was preceded by another, diametrically opposed, conception which depicted Buddhism as a formidable "worship of nothingness."

Nirvāna is a Sanskrit word that refers to the ultimate state reached by the Buddha. It contrasts with *samsāra*, the cycle of life and death. While *nirvāna* in principle remains the ultimate goal of Buddhism, it has lost the negative connotations it held during the nineteenth century. In the Hīnayāna tradition, *nirvāna* was defined as the extinction of all desires, a pure absence.

The Mahāyāna tradition, however, went further, triggering a mental revolution: the indefinable *nirvāna* is now defined according to four terms: permanence, bliss, subjectivity, and purity. The ultimate goal is reinterpreted as "Enlightenment" or, better still, "Awakening" (a term used to translate the Sanskrit word *bodhi*, the experience whereby one becomes a "buddha" or "awakened one"). It is a pure experience which, rather than putting an end to the world of the senses, sanctifies it and assumes a place within this world. Far from rejecting the world, Awakening becomes a form of supreme bliss within this world, cleansed of all its negative aspects and false perceptions caused by illusion. As the layman

Vimalakīrti says to the *arhat* Shariputra, who is complaining about living in an overly imperfect world: "When your mind is pure, the world becomes a Pure Land."

Given the historical importance of the "nihilistic" conception of Buddhism in the West, it would be useful to quickly trace the development of this idea. While it was generally recognized that Buddhists consider *nirvāna* to represent deliverance, the end of a painful transmigration, opinions were divided as regards the nature of this deliverance. Some thought that the Buddhist rejection of the soul and of God mean that *nirvāna* must involve total destruction and that Buddhism is therefore nihilism, a somber form of pessimism. Others have wisely sought to define Buddhism as agnosticism, arguing that the Buddha did not comment on the nature of this deliverance. Both sides evidently considered it difficult to understand why Buddhists equate *nirvāna* with beatitude and immortality and why they claim that the Buddha overcame death.

There can be little doubt that the person who contributed most to the nihilist interpretation of *nirvāna* during the nineteenth century was the German philosopher Hegel. For him, the Buddhist *nirvāna* is simply nothingness, "which Buddhists make the principle of everything, the final goal and the ultimate end of everything." He therefore considered it completely natural that the Buddha should be represented adopting a "thinking posture" in which "feet and hands are intertwined with a toe entering the mouth." This is the perfect expression of a "withdrawal into oneself, sucking on oneself." However, according to Hegel, Buddhist nothingness is not the opposite of being, as it becomes later, but is instead the absolute, free from all determination. Shifting to the absolute destroys one's relative and conditioned individuality; the emptiness that results is not nothing, it is merely another name for plenitude.

Unfortunately, heirs of Hegel have only retained the formulation and not the subtle nuances. Even the eminent French scholar Eugène Burnouf, the first translator of the *Lotus Sutra*, stated that the Buddha "saw supreme good in the annihilation of the thinking principle." His disciple Jules Barthélémy Saint-Hilaire went one step further, stating: "If there were ever anything in the world which goes against Christian doctrine, it is this deplorable idea of annihilation which forms the basis of Buddhism." This is why the Buddha was subsequently referred to as the "great Christ of emptiness" (Edgar Quinet) and Buddhism as a "Church of nihilism" (Ernest Renan).

The German philosopher Schopenhauer brought a more fundamentally pessimistic slant to Buddhism. He considered Buddhism to be an atheistic religion. All the same, *nirvāna* is not a nothingness in itself; it only appears that way to us due to the powerlessness of language and thought. Schopenhauer's views, in *The World as Will and Representation*, are similar to those of Hegel on this point when he writes: "Defining Nirwana [*sic*] as nothingness amounts to saying that *samsāra* does not contain a single element which could serve to define or construct Nirwana." Nietzsche, on the other hand, sees in Buddhism a "nostalgia for nothingness", an "asthenia of the will" and states that "tragedy must save us from Buddhism."

The nihilist theory rests on two fallacies: one is an error regarding the goal, namely *nirvāna*, the transcendental nature of which falls beyond any possible formulation yet has been interpreted as simple inexistence or annihilation; the other is an error relating to the dialectical method of the Mādhyamika which proceeds according to negation, but does not stop at negation, and which dismisses all notions, even that of emptiness. This simply means that we cannot say anything about ultimate reality; it does not mean that reality does not exist beyond or outside of what we can say.

According to Roger-Pol Droit, this misunderstanding, which lasted throughout the nineteenth century and beyond, is symptomatic of the evils of Western society; it reveals in particular the fears of Western philosophers when faced with the specter of nihilism. This extended beyond a simple yet regrettable inability to understand a doctrine too different from our own; it also represented an actual political strategy, an active form of resistance against the radical evils which appeared to be threatening Western society. The European conscience projected its own fears onto Buddhism due to the "death of God," a loss of metaphysical anchorage in post-Kantian philosophy, uprisings among the working classes, and the "decline of the West," amongst other things.

Other socio-political factors have also played a part, most notably the rise of colonialism and of the missionary spirit. According to Droit, the philosophical judgment about India seems to reach a turning point with Barthélémy Saint-Hilaire, the author of a virulent pamphlet against Buddhism entitled *The Buddha and his Religion*. It is no coincidence that this scholar was also Minister for Foreign Affairs in the cabinet of Jules Ferry during the Third Republic and France's colonial expansion.

The growing indifference to India during the second half of the nineteenth century – after the enthusiasm of the "Oriental Renaissance" in the first part of that century – is a mystery to historians. The change brought about by the gradual idealization of Buddhism from the start of the twentieth century should, logically speaking, have sparked renewed interest in the philosophy of India. However, this did not occur, perhaps because the Buddhism in question was no longer perceived to be Indian, first and foremost. The debate surrounding *nirvāna* therefore seems to be a symptom as well as a cause of misunderstanding where Buddhism is concerned.

—— "Buddhism is a philosophy, —— not a religion"

Buddhism is essentially an attitude to life, what you could call, for want of a better phrase, a philosophy, but a philosophy that tends towards the absolute.
Michel Malherbe, *The Religions of Mankind*, 1990

This is undoubtedly the most widespread idea relating to Buddhism, even among academics. According to Jean-François Revel in *The Monk and the Philosopher*, "This is a philosophy

27

comprising a particularly important metaphysical dimension. This metaphysical dimension, however, forms part of the philosophy and does not derive from a revelation, even though it does involve ritualistic aspects which are associated with religious practice."

For many, however, the essence of Buddhism boils down to a singular "logical revolt" against revelation or metaphysics in any form. However, what applies to certain schools of Buddhism, which have rather too quickly been labeled as "primitive Buddhism," does not necessarily apply to Buddhism in its entirety. Even early Buddhism is always derived and plural.

Buddhist philosophy, of course, boasts names such as Nāgārjuna or Chandrakirti (sixth century) in India, Tsongkhapa (fourteenth century) in Tibet, Jizang (549–623), Fazang (643–712) or Zongmi (774–841) in China and Kūkai (774–835) or Dōgen (1200–53) in Japan. The logical or epistomological arguments put forward by Buddhist scholars are certainly no less valid than those proposed by their Western colleagues. However, they always fall within a particular framework which is that of Buddhist deliverance rather than that of universal reason. As the Belgian scholar Louis de la Vallée-Poussin notes, Buddhism "was born of and has lived on the belief in the afterlife and in the retribution for actions, on faith in eternal salvation ... To make it a form of rationalism would be to prevent oneself from understanding anything about it" (*Bouddhisme: Opinions sur l'histoire de la dogmatique*, 1925).

Some have avoided the two terms "religion" and "philosophy" altogether by using the words "spirituality" or "wisdom" instead. And, for others, Buddhism is first and foremost a path that leads to Awakening, or a moral doctrine founded on compassion. In reality, these definitions are anything but neutral: it is always about claiming, in all innocence, that Buddhism is *not* a religion or at least that its specifically religious aspects are of secondary importance.

When addressing the philosophical aspect of Buddhism, it is often said that "reality is unknowable." This negative statement relates both to the nature of things or reality and to knowledge. If things do not exist in themselves, as stated by the Mahāyāna tradition, can the nature of things really be the object of knowledge? If the ultimate truth is ineffable, and cannot be conceptualized, knowledge must be non-conceptual and non-linguistic.

At the moment of Awakening, the Buddha is said to have achieved omniscience, a knowledge of all the *dharmas* or elements constituting reality. In early Buddhism, this knowledge is based on a discursive approach. There is, however, an "inconceivable" domain (*achintya*), which thought cannot reach. This may explain why the Buddha rejected certain questions relating, for example, to the origin of the world, which have no soteriological value. The term *achintya* was therefore originally used to refer to badly formulated questions. It subsequently came to denote the very nature of reality and the paradoxical perception of nature within Awakening.

The epistemological status of knowledge in the most ancient of the texts is somewhat ambiguous. Numerous texts state that there are two kinds of obstacle to Awakening – passion and knowledge. All empirical knowledge, being conditioned, bears the stamp of illusion. As an element of personality, consciousness (*vijñāna*) is transitory and painful. Rational thought is therefore not a supreme faculty that legislates on all things, as claimed by Descartes.

There is, however, an intuitive form of knowledge which is not subject to these limitations. Since the earliest centuries of Buddhism, certain texts have deemed thought to be more stable, describing it as "luminous" and as the *dharma* that encompasses everything. During the development of Mahāyāna over the first few centuries of the Common Era, this knowledge came to be defined as a kind of gnosis (*prajñā*). The question is therefore to identify whether it prolongs discursive knowledge or whether it in fact contradicts it.

More specifically, the idea emerges that the apprehension of the absolute is achieved through a particular form of knowledge known as *prajñāpāramitā* or Perfection of Wisdom. This paradoxical knowledge is, in fact, non-knowledge. The apophatic or negative approach sees Awakening as inconceivable, inexpressible, and unreachable. It can only be approached through a dialectical double negation (neither this nor that) or, ultimately, through silence.

In the *Vimalakīrti Sutra*, the layman Vimalakīrti declares: "All *dharmas* are devoid of marks and as such are inexpressible and unthinkable. Being inexistent, they are devoid of marks. We cannot say anything about them or, if we do, it is solely through convention. To know them is not to think about them." As a result, practitioners are supposed to perceive all things like a reflection in a mirror, water in a mirage, sound in an echo, vision in a dream – or, more metaphorically, like the erection of a eunuch or the pregnancy of an infertile woman. Awakening, says Vimalakīrti, is not confirmed either by the body or by thought; it is the end of all false views.

The same idea can be found in a famous *prajñāpāramitā* text, the *Heart Sutra*. In this very short text, recited daily by Buddhists from Tibet to Japan, the bodhisattva Avalokiteshvara explains emptiness to the Arhat Shariputra. The latter represents the naive viewpoint of the Hīnayāna and learns, to his great surprise, that all of the traditional dogma is null and void when it comes to the ultimate reality. This is notably the case with the Four Noble Truths (relating to suffering, the origin of suffering, the extinction of suffering or *nirvāna*, and the path to achieving this), pronounced by the Buddha during his first sermon. Somewhat paradoxically, this eminently philosophical text ends with a mantra. This has not escaped the attention of commentators: some have seen this as simple interpolation and others as a new form of language adapted to Emptiness, a foretaste of the "intentional" language of Tantric Buddhism.

The ideas of the *Vimalakīrti Sutra* have been adopted and systematized by the so-called Middle Way school or Mādhyamika, as expressed by Nāgārjuna during the third century CE. Nāgārjuna inherited the *prajñāpāramitā* literature and is considered to be its first systematizer. He was very influential, and his work constitutes an essential and unavoidable reference point for many commentators, the ultimate orthodoxy in Mahāyāna doctrine.

Nāgārjuna logically demonstrates the futility of any particular knowledge. He presents the unthinkable nature of reality in the form of a classic tetralemma. As the etymology of the word indicates, this tetralemma is composed of four propositions: affirmation (X = A), negation (X = non-A), synthesis of the two (X = A *and* non-A) and dialectical negation of the two (X = *neither* A *nor* non-A). The third statement clearly contradicts the law of non-contradiction as defined by Aristotelian logic. Whatever the case, absolute reality, by definition, escapes these four propositions insofar as they define all possible relationships.

The agnosticism of Mādhyamika Buddhism is not simply Pyrrhonian-like skepticism. Neither is it nihilism, as its refutation of existence does not imply non-existence. The value of this intellectual deconstruction is expressed in colorful terms in a later text, the *Hevajra tantra*. In D. L. Snellgrove's translation: "Just as a man who suffers with flatulence is given beans to eat, so that wind may overcome wind in the way of a homoeopathic cure, so existence is purified by existence in the countering of discursive thought by its own kind" (p. 93). Even since the publication of T. R. V. Murti's classic book, *The Central Philosophy of Buddhism* (1955), Mādhyamika Buddhism has been considered the ultimate outcome in Buddhist thought. This has encouraged a purely philosophical reading of early Buddhism that tends to reduce the Buddha to a precursor of Wittgenstein or, in other words, to someone who rejects metaphysical questions by demonstrating that they are poorly formulated and boil down in general to grammatical error.

By denying the real existence of the self and of things, Mādhyamika seemed to be undermining one of the fundamental aspects of the Buddhist doctrine – the principle of retribution of acts or karma. To avoid this pitfall, Nāgārjuna resorts to the notion of the Two Truths. Insofar as the conventional truth represents the only means of accessing the ultimate truth (Emptiness), all traditional practices retain their raison d'être for the time being. However certain epigones of Nāgārjuna, taking the logic of Emptiness to its limit, have purely and simply denied all forms of mediation and most notably all values in their cognitive approach to reality. This applies, for example, to the most radical forms of Chan Buddhism.

In theory, Chan (Zen) derives from Mādhyamika. An early Chan text refers for instance to Nāgārjuna's tetralemma as follows: "Can Awakening be obtained through being?" – "No." – "Through non-being?" – "No." – "Through being *and* non-being?" – "No." "Through *neither* being *nor* non-being?" – "No." – "So how can we grasp its meaning?" "Nothing can be grasped; this is what we call obtaining Awakening."

The ninth-century master Linji Yixuan, founder of the Linji (Japanese: Rinzai) sect that went on to become one of the two largest schools in Japanese Zen, described knowledge as a "cataract on the eye" and its objects as "flowers in the sky," that is, ophthalmological illusions. He provides his own version of the tetralemma, describing the relationship between the knowing subject and the object as follows: "At times one takes away the person but does not take away the environment. At times one takes away the environment but does not take away the person. At times one takes away both the person and the environment. At times one takes away neither the person nor the environment." When a disciple asks him to elaborate on this first point, he responds with a cryptic poem: "Warm sun shines forth, spreading the earth with brocade. The little child's hair hangs down, white as silk thread." He does the same for the other propositions. While his replies are subject to doctrinal hermeneutics, this change in register radically modifies the "philosophical" value of Nāgārjuna's tetralemma by allocating an oracle-like nature to the language.

Although it is important to view Buddhism within a general philosophical framework, the cost of doing so should also be questioned. Indeed, by failing to question the privilege granted to a certain type of Western rationalist discourse, we risk contributing to a new and more subtle form of exclusion, again shifting the question to the West. By placing Buddhist thought within a philosophical context, we are making a choice which – however justifiable – has various consequences. For one thing, it implies an exclusion of the non-philosophical – which is judged to be less relevant in terms of understanding another culture or at least in evoking Western sympathy towards other cultures.

This exclusion undoubtedly aims to avoid labeling Buddhism as a trend in spirituality, wisdom, or religiosity or, worse still, a cult. Although driven by different motivations, our distinct preference for a philosophical Buddhism links in with attempts by Asian elites to present a purified, "demythologized," and rational form of Buddhism – in short, a doctrine perfectly adapted to modernity. This minimal doctrine also offers a means of controlling the proliferation of discourse. It involves a certain rejection of the diversity of practices and beliefs in the name of intellectual orthodoxy.

It is undoubtedly neither possible nor desirable to settle the question once and for all. If we limit ourselves here to traditional Buddhism or, in other words, Asian Buddhism, this could be defined as a religion, despite being quite different from the types of religion we are used to, a religion with important philosophical, spiritual, and magical components – all terms which our Western logic would deem to be mutually exclusive.

If we stick to the definition proposed by sociologist Émile Durkheim in *The Elementary Forms of the Religious Life* (1912), Buddhism is indeed a religion in terms of being a "system of beliefs and practices relating to the sacred which produces social behaviors and unites all the individuals who adhere to it within the same community."

Why not simply stick to Buddhist "thought" – a broader term which has the advantage of including ritual logic and mythology?

We are indeed dealing here with thought in its broader sense. True, it is a form of thought determined by a given society and culture, yet what thought isn't? All philosophy, however pure, is cultural in the sense that it reflects the linguistic categories of the language in which it is expressed.

——— "All Buddhists are seeking ——— to achieve Awakening"

The spiritual goal which Buddhism strives to achieve is Awakening.
Matthieu Ricard, *The Monk and the Philosopher*, 1997

With Mahāyāna Buddhism emerges a new ideal, that of the bodhisattva, that is, the practitioner who seeks to reach Awakening, or has already reached it. Awakening does not imply, like *nirvāna*, withdrawal from the sensory world; quite the contrary. The term "bodhisattva" now signifies an Awakened being who is fully alive, in this world or in others.

The ideal of the bodhisattva has come into competition with that of the *arhat*: from the ascetic living outside this world to the saint living in it. This new ideal evidently implies a critique of the ancient. According to the tenants of Mahāyāna Buddhism, the *arhat* practices only for himself, to reach *nirvāna* as quickly as possible, while the bodhisattva, in his great compassion, aspires to become a buddha only to guide all other beings towards Awakening, and refuses salvation if it is only individual. There is an emphasis, now, no longer on a sort of passive sainthood characterized by renunciation, but on active virtues (the Six Perfections: generosity, patience, energy, morality, concentration, and wisdom) that are more actively adapted to the needs of ordinary people. As such, the "career" of bodhisattva is no longer limited to monks, but is also open to laypeople, men and women alike. The ultimate goal has also been modified: it is no longer sainthood resulting in *nirvāna*, but a perfect and supreme awakening put to the service of attaining salvation for everyone in this world.

According to certain Mahāyāna texts such as the *Lotus Sutra,* the path of the bodhisattva is the only true one: all others are simply expedients, pious lies that allow one to reach this unique reality. And so there is only one true "vehicle," the Great Vehicle – all others are only illusions. There are two crucial moments in the "career" of a bodhisattva: the initial thought of Awakening (*bodhicitta*) and the final stage at which supreme Awakening is obtained. Although these two moments can be separated by fantastically lengthy intervals of time (in the scale of many lives), the final moment is already contained in the initial moment. This initial moment is therefore extremely important, because it is then that the believer makes the wish, not only to reach Awakening, but to delay it until all beings are saved. It is this spirit of compassion which will guide the believer in his practice, thus smoothing out all difficulties.

Although the term "bodhisattva" can in theory be applied to any adept of the Mahāyāna, it primarily designates those particularly glorious beings who, after long periods of practice, have accumulated many merits that can now be put to the service of others. These bodhisattvas have the power to manifest themselves in any form (divine, human, or animal) to help those in need. They appear even among the damned in hell or take an animal form to help animals. For this reason, bodhisattvas quickly became the object of a cult that transformed Buddhism into a religion based on faith and devotion.

But let's come back to the topic of "ordinary" bodhisattvas. With the development of the Mahāyāna school in China or in Japan, the Mahāyāna monks came to redefine monastic discipline to adapt it to new cultural conditions. The emphasis was now placed on interiorized ethics based upon faith and altruism. It was no longer sufficient to simply avoid evil, one must now be good. There has developed, as a result, a new type of ordination, founded on the precepts called "Bodhisattva precepts" and open to laymen (and particularly to the great patrons of Buddhism). These newly ordained bodhisattvas turn to social works, such as the construction of temples, hospices, roads, and bridges.

There is no shortage of canonical texts or established practices to assert that Awakening is the ultimate goal of the practice of Buddhism. Some would say that this goal is far from reach given the weaknesses of humans, yet that, in the short term at least, practicing Buddhist virtues, even in an imperfect state of mind, enables the individual to accumulate certain merits. This positive karma, it is said, translates into certain benefits in the present life or a better rebirth in the future. An individual may, for example, be given the chance to be reborn as a human, preferably a male, and into a good family.

The idea that Awakening is the ultimate goal boasts a certain degree of nobility compared to the popular conception of karma. Nevertheless the fact remains that, for the vast majority of Buddhists in Asia, this notion of Awakening is too often used as a convenient alibi to disguise the fact that the real practice seeks first and foremost to obtain worldly benefits, whether material (such as prosperity) or symbolic (such as prestige). We risk not understanding anything about real-life Buddhism if we underestimate these "human, too human" motivations. Buddhists often live according to expedients which are said to be "salvific." These expedients, or "skillful means" (*upāya*), tend to become an end in themselves, while Awakening recedes into an increasingly more distant future.

Laypeople primarily seek to obtain tangible benefits such as happiness, prestige, or wealth, or to obtain slightly less tangible benefits immediately: the salvation of a loved one in the afterlife, for example. Awakening remains the confessed goal of clerics although, in practice, most monastic communities are also seeking material prosperity or renown in this world and greater recognition in the next. Add to this a number of "superpowers": the ability to read other people's thoughts, clairvoyance, and so on. Those who possess these "powers" are accorded greater respect, thus indirectly making a significant contribution to their material prosperity.

While these goals may seem somewhat less ambitious than Awakening, we should not be too hasty and condemn them as reflecting a decline or degeneration of the primitive ideal. Instead, we should consider them a sort of ruse of Buddhist reason, a means of Buddhism establishing itself in the long term. In fact, ever since it was first established, Buddhism has had to make compromises to survive as an institution. Judging by the Vinaya texts, which give a detailed account of the disciplinary rules decreed by the Buddha, the first community was not a gathering of glorious *arhats* but rather a group of quite ordinary people. Nevertheless, this group formed the basis for an institution which has survived for centuries and kept the flame of Awakening alive, albeit somewhat dimmed.

However, it is not simply resignation or the abandonment of an overly ambitious or far-removed ideal that drives most Buddhists to concentrate on the present or near future. There are also spiritual reasons for this in many cases. In fact, by concentrating too heavily on Awakening and the brighter future it offers, we risk bypassing what is most important – the present and the human condition. In certain schools of Mahāyāna Buddhism, Awakening is no longer a goal in itself; it is more a question of achieving balance between Awakening and skillful means. After all, the *Vimalakīrti Sutra* states that wisdom without expedients is no better than expedients without wisdom. Wisdom without expedients remains a dead letter; it is no longer able to help others. The reverse is also true.

So what are these pervasive expedients? Ritual, first and foremost. Ritual is even omnipresent within sects that claim to be anti-ritualistic, such as Zen. Zen ritual refers, not only to rites in the literal sense of the word (prayer, reciting the scriptures, icon worship, etc.), but also the smallest of actions in everyday life (meals, work, etc.). This blurring of distinctions between the sacred and profane spheres is perhaps the sought-after goal. As one Zen master puts it: "Awakening that is aware of itself is Awakening in a dream."

Awakening continues to be presented as the mark of "authentic" Buddhism, while the concern for the "worldly benefits" (*genze riyaku* in Japanese) derived from pious works and the worship of Buddhist deities is dismissed as a less genuine form of Buddhism, the result of a lame compromise with local culture and popular needs. It would be presumptuous, however, for us Westerners to assume that we can easily identify and understand the true teaching of the Buddha after centuries of oblivion and deviations, while arguing that the people of Asia, who practiced it for such a long time, never really understood it. This kind of assumption reveals the resilience of the Orientalist ideology among Western adherents of Buddhism (or rather, Neo-Buddhism). Although we no longer disparage Buddhism in the name of an alleged Western cultural superiority, as our forefathers did, our tendency to idealize it and to reduce it to a teaching untainted by worldly concerns and focused exclusively on Awakening remains fundamentally mistaken.

It was not the expectation of Awakening that convinced Chinese, Tibetan, and Japanese leaders to convert to Buddhism but rather the protection Buddhism appeared to offer them against evils of all kinds, both individual and collective (epidemics, invasions, etc.). The success of Buddhism in Asia is primarily due to its presumed effectiveness in protecting the state. An essential part of the monks' activities was to pray for the health of the emperor and the prosperity of the people.

So why all the fuss about Awakening? And what kind of Awakening are we talking about anyway? Like *nirvāna*, Awakening is famously difficult to define. Is it, as is often said, a sort of rediscovery of our profound inner self or, on the other hand, the realization of its non-existence? In Zen, in particular, all beings are essentially awakened by virtue of their buddha nature. Nothing can be done to enhance their perfection: One Zen master said that the hope of achieving Awakening through practice is a bit like wanting to add a head on top of one's own head.

The very notion of Awakening has evolved considerably. To cite one example: the ordained Buddhists of East Asia add the patronym Shākya before their religious name to indicate that they are, symbolically, the sons and daughters of Shākyamuni (the "Sage of the Shākya"), i.e. the Buddha. In other words, once they have undergone ordination they are ritually affiliated with the lineage of the Buddha, their common ancestor (and their ordination charter bears the name of "blood line" – despite the fact that this is mostly a purely symbolic affiliation). In that sense, Awakening is not so much the result of a spiritual quest but of their inalienable heritage as descendants of the Buddha. Buddhist sects and movements in China and Japan were once called "families." In this family context, it is ordination and not practice which provides an entitlement to Awakening.

———— "Buddhism teaches the ———— impermanence of all things"

The Dhamma, the universal moral law discovered by the Buddha, is summarized in the Four Noble Truths.
Mahathera, "The Essence of the Buddha's Teachings," in
Présence du Bouddhisme, 2008

The search for a core universal Buddhism tends to focus on the Four Noble Truths pronounced by the Buddha during his first sermon in Benares. Those who claim that Buddhism represents a kind of stoic wisdom based on asceticism refer to these truths.

The first truth relates to suffering (*dukha*, a term which designates the acute feeling of universal impermanence) and is described as follows: birth is suffering, old age is suffering, illness is suffering, death is suffering, contact with something one does not like is suffering, separation from something one does like is suffering, failure to achieve one's desire is suffering; to summarize, the five types of object of attachment are suffering.

The second truth teaches the origin of suffering, "thirst" (*trishna*) which leads us from life to life, accompanied by pleasure and desire: a thirst for pleasure and thirst for existence as well as thirst for non-existence.

The third truth teaches the suppression of suffering through the complete destruction of desire. This suppression of all desire and all pain is known as *nirvāna*.

The fourth truth teaches the Eightfold Path (*mārga*) to stopping pain. It constitutes the Buddhist soteriology or "doctrine of salvation." The Eightfold Path that makes it up was defined by the Buddha as a middle way that avoids the two extremes: the pleasures of the senses and asceticism. The route comprises eight branches based on morality or *shīla* (pure language, pure action, pure means of existence), concentration or *samādhi* (pure application, pure memory, pure meditation), and wisdom or *prajña* (pure faith, pure desire).

In short, the desire or "thirst" for living and being happy clashes with the impermanence of all things and as such is a source of pain. This desire, based on ignorance – the unrealistic perception of a substantial and autonomous self – leads us to commit acts for which there is an automatic retribution (karma) which causes us to constantly fall back into the painful cycle of birth and death, or *samsāra*. The only way of breaking this vicious cycle is to cut the root of desire. To achieve this, a long process of purification is required. The state thereby achieved, the total extinction of the fires of desire, is *nirvāna*.

The formulation of the Four Noble Truths, perhaps judged too simple in its pragmatism by some, soon developed in a complex doctrinal system, primarily psychological and moral. The world in which we live, our environment, and our selves are determined by our karma – our past actions – as well. Between our past, present, and future lives exists a causal chain, ordinarily described as consisting of twelve links whose root is ignorance. From this we successively derive the psychic constructions, consciousness, the "name-and-form" (or personality), the six sensorial domains, touch, sensation, the "thirst" (particularly sexual desire), attachment to the self, existence, birth (or rather, rebirth), old age, and death. This twelve-link chain describes the evolution of five aggregates in three existences: the first two describe the past existence, the next seven the present existence, and the last three the future existence. This series, however, is reversible: while the series described above represents the normal process of existence, the inverted sequence describes a return to the source which allows one, by reaching back to the causes, to suppress the effects and end the process.

This essentially psychological schema of the "dependent origination" is accompanied by another, of a more cosmic and mythological nature: that of the six possible destinies which await us after the present life – that of the damned (the Buddhist hells), of the animals, of the hungry ghosts, of the *asura* (a kind of Titan), of humans, and of the *devas* (celestial beings). It is always a human, in the end, who is reborn in an infernal, animal, or celestial state, only human life, with its mix of suffering and joy, can break with the vicious cycle of births and deaths. Indeed, only in human form can one's karma be radically modified – all other forms are subject to the retributions of past karma. It is primarily this second schema that influenced the ulterior development of Buddhism, notably in China and in Japan, by allowing the emergence of a mythological description of the afterlife (with hells and paradises).

There is no denying the fact that these Four Noble Truths summarize the philosophy of the earliest form of Buddhism, if not that of the Buddha himself, and that they continued to play an important role in the two main forms of Buddhism which developed subsequently, the Mahāyāna and the Hīnāyāna. Despite this, these Four Truths were quickly relativized in various schools of the Mahāyāna, most notably in the tradition known as the Perfection of Wisdom (*prajñāpāramitā*). This tradition teaches that everything is empty and devoid of its own substance. In this emptiness, suffering does not exist in itself, which is therefore all the more reason to eliminate it.

In one of the most widely regarded texts of this tradition, the *Heart Sutra*, these Four Noble Truths are actually called into question. In this text, the bodhisattva Avalokiteshvara declares to the *arhat* Shariputra that in ultimate reality, or emptiness, all things are empty of their own nature – starting with the self. As a result, there is neither ignorance nor an extinction of ignorance; no aging or death and no elimination of aging or death. This boils down to saying that in emptiness, the Four Noble Truths are no longer relevant: there is no suffering, no origin of suffering, no extinction of suffering, no pathway to extinguishing suffering.

What seems to be questioned in this text, in the name of a superior truth, is the very existence of Hīnayāna Buddhism. Likewise, the great Mahāyāna thinker Nāgārjuna claims to prove the unrealistic nature of karmic retribution, transmigration (*samsāra*), suffering, and deliverance. He does not consider the Four Truths to be noble truths but rather insufficient half-truths that must be transcended through his dialectical method. Yet they remain indispensable as a preliminary approach, just like the conventional truth is indispensable to reach the ultimate truth. Because, he adds, "emptiness, when misunderstood, destroys those whose intelligence is mediocre, much like a weakly held snake or poorly applied magic."

A radical change of ideal is therefore evident within the Mahāyāna: the ultimate goal is no longer *nirvāna*, which is considered to be too negative and individualist; instead it is Awakening or *bodhi*, which enables bodhisattvas to "leave the world" while still remaining in it and to work with compassion towards the salvation of all beings.

This Awakening is possible because all beings possess a buddha nature. We therefore arrive at the notion of "fundamental Awakening" (in Japanese *hongaku*) according to which every being is essentially perfect and pure and therefore purification is useless or even harmful. Purification, in fact, contributes to the illusion and therefore to suffering, whereas the only thing which matters is to dissipate this illusion at once.

This illusion is the result of dualist thought. Conversely, the non-dualist thought of Mahāyāna Buddhism denies any duality between *samsāra* and *nirvāna* or between passion and Awakening. In the Hīnayāna, *nirvāna* is defined as the opposite of *samsāra*, whereas in Mahāyāna it is identified with *samsāra*. According to the latter view, this world is only a "valley of tears" on the face of it; in reality it is perfect *nirvāna*. Similarly, the distinction between common people and buddhas is no longer as clear-cut. All beings are already buddhas in terms of their actions and powers.

This conception, while it confirms everyday realities, contrasts with the negation of the world which characterizes early Buddhism. When it comes to iconography, this is reflected in the contrast between the Indian Buddha, emaciated and somber, and the popular "Laughing Buddha" of the Chinese, who is obese and beaming. The contrast is evidently less entrenched in practice, although the two images reveal a major change in the Mahāyānist conception of man and the world, compared to the Hīnayāna conception.

The development of Tantric Buddhism takes things a step further still. In fact this tradition, strongly influenced by Indian yoga, ends with the human body becoming sacred and a reevaluation of desire. Man, like all things, emanates from a divine principle, a cosmic Buddha, to whom it is sufficient to return. Nature is no longer regarded as a world of illusion which should be rejected at all costs, but rather a world of realization, the river of bliss in which we all, as living beings, bathe. Instead of being based on illusion and suffering, which are wrongly held to be real, it is sufficient to focus on Awakening, which is our source, so that suffering loses all substance, all ontological reality. This notion is far removed from the ascetic vision of Buddhism and the Four Noble Truths, which continue to be cited as if through a misguided sense of obligation.

——— "The belief in karma leads ———
to fatalism"

Everyday experience familiarises us with the facts which are grouped under the name of heredity ... The Indian philosophers called character, as thus defined, "karma." It is this karma which passed from life to life and linked them in the chain of transmigrations.

Aldous Huxley

The term "karma" is one of the very few Sanskrit terms to have passed into common vocabulary. According to the *Petit Robert* French dictionary, it means "act" and designates the "central dogma of Hindu religion according to which all actions and intentions are inscribed in the destiny of living beings (a sort of predestination)." According to this view, Buddhism has therefore borrowed one of its central concepts from Hinduism, modifying the concept somewhat over time.

Buddhist karma is the law of retribution for acts. Every action is perceived as a cause that brings about an effect: the effect will follow on irreversibly from the cause. It is, however, the intention that determines the act. Each one of us is responsible for his or her own actions and each current action is itself determined by a long series of past acts. It is this which gives the notion of karma a hint of fatalism. However, the action is never entirely determined; there is always an element of free will involved. The individual is always faced with a choice that will have good or bad consequences. Nothing is ever entirely determined.

In the earliest Buddhist texts, karmic retribution was portrayed as being inevitable and highly individualized. The individual faces his actions alone and cannot escape their consequences, whatever he does. Karma, in particular, explains the requirement for rebirth: the weight of one's actions constitutes an individual's destiny and affects his or her rebirth on one of the Six Paths (*gati*).

In the *Samyutta-nikāya*, the Buddha states: "The death of a mother or a sister, the death of a father, a son, a daughter, the loss of relatives, of possessions, all this you have experienced over the long ages. *Samsāra* is without beginning and without end ... So over the long ages you have suffered pain, misfortune and you have nourished the ground of cemeteries; long enough, in truth, to become tired with existence, long enough to want to escape from all this."

The principle of karmic retribution is clear: humans are invariably followed by their actions which catch up with them sooner or later – "just as the calf finds its mother in a herd of a thousand cows." The mechanisms of karma, however, are somewhat complicated. At first sight, karma seems to involve a degree of fatalism given that psychic inertia leads some to perdition and others to divine joy. However, the structure of the system ensures that a degree of karma remains at all times which leads back to the human condition sooner or later – perceived to be the center of gravity for the system. Suffering eventually drives beings away from evil, whereas too much pleasure causes them to succumb to the temptations of evil.

Living beings go from one existence to another and their condition is determined by the merits or faults of their actions and not, as stated in Brahmanism, by sacrifice and ritual in general. Early Buddhism focuses on the moral value of the action and rejects ritualism and the worshiping of gods. Each individual is responsible for his or her actions and no one can do anything to help anyone else. This austere notion underwent fundamental modifications with the emergence of the transfer of merits theory, which has become an important feature of Mahāyāna Buddhism. In the latter, those who have accumulated a surplus of merits can share these merits with other less perfect individuals. This conception underlies the worshiping of the bodhisattvas, compassionate beings who delay their entry into *nirvāna* in order to save others.

The keystone of the system – the notion of deliverance – is situated outside of the logic of retribution. Salvation is not achieved through merit alone; it involves the radical abandonment of all acts, both religious and profane. According to this viewpoint, *samsāra* and *nirvāna* – life, death, and immortality – are merely false notions. This view of the ultimate truth is summarized in the Hridaya sutra, the epitome of Mahāyāna doctrine.

The Buddhist dogma relating to the absence of a soul or self makes transmigration something of a paradox: what is it that transmigrates if the self is simply an illusory series of states of consciousness which disappear into death? What is the point in practicing and accumulating merit if this self does not reap the rewards? Clearly this notion goes against the notion of karmic retribution. To rectify this, the notion of an "intermediary being" was developed, a sort of personal conscience at the junction between two existences. The orthodox solution, however, consisted in stating that, while there are actions, there is no agent or subject, no permanent entity behind them.

The conception of the afterlife presented by Buddhism was undoubtedly one of the main contributors to its success in Asian societies. In early Buddhism, retribution for acts was a semi-automatic process which could affect an individual during his or her lifetime as well as determining subsequent rebirths. This theory was subsequently subject to heavy modification as part of the general development of the Buddhist doctrine. The idea is that humans can influence their destiny through their efforts and the acts they commit during life on earth. Retribution for actions remains one of the key elements of the system, although the individual is no longer solely responsible. Others can also use merits they have accumulated to benefit the deceased, hence the increasing importance of rituals in generating benefits which can easily be transferred to another person. This is notably the case with funeral rituals which enable the deceased to be assigned merits which they did not manage to accumulate during their life on earth, therefore ensuring the deceased final deliverance, entry into paradise, or simply a better rebirth.

In Tibetan Buddhism, the deceased has to wander in the intermediary world (*bardo*) for some time before being reborn. The famous *Tibetan Book of the Dead*, which was read at the bedside of the deceased to guide them during this journey and explain to them the dangers and temptations they would encounter on the way, sought to ensure the deceased the best possible rebirth. Where Chinese Buddhism is concerned, the conception of the other world underwent a significant development with the theory of the Ten Kings of Hell and in particular the court of King Yama, where the deceased are judged based on their past actions and have to undergo a kind of purgatory before they can be reborn. The funeral rituals carried out in the name of the deceased by descendants play a crucial role at this stage and can influence the judgment passed. These rituals lead the deceased towards rebirth over a period of seven weeks during which they roam between the two worlds.

In Mahāyāna Buddhism in particular, salvation can also be obtained through the intercession of bodhisattvas who have accumulated various merits during their lifetime. The intercession of Avalokiteshvara (known as Guanyin in Chinese and Kannon in Japanese) and Kshitigarbha (Dizang in Chinese, Jizō in Japanese) is said to be particularly effective.

Salvation can also be provided by certain buddhas, such as Amitābha, who, before achieving Awakening, vowed to save all beings who invoke him. Finally, in certain schools of Buddhism, karmic retribution is sometimes undermined by the notion of effective ritual or by certain practices such as meditation. The Zen school, for example, often features accounts of conversion whereby a demonic spirit is converted by the teachings of a Zen master and suddenly realizes the truth of emptiness, thereby escaping his bad karma.

Indian Buddhism saw deliverance at the end of many of rebirths during which individuals would gradually accumulate merits enabling them to be reborn in human form initially and then to convert to Buddhism so as to progress toward the goal. Chinese and Japanese Buddhism come to assert the notion that Awakening or deliverance is possible in this very life and that everyone can "become a buddha in this very body."

Another trend which has developed in Mahāyāna Buddhism with the notion of Emptiness is the idea that sins are empty and devoid of reality, in other words, that all karma is null and void. All that is needed is to realize its true nature, its fundamental non-existence, to rid oneself of all defilements. "In the absolute, karma is empty." The problem is that people live in the relative, and here, karma is indeed real. Tradition warns us against the dangers and deviations that could be caused by the notion of an empty karma. This notion was indeed blamed for legitimizing a transgression of traditional morals in the name of a practice allegedly transcending good and evil.

Buddhism has sometimes been accused – in particular during the colonial period – of encouraging social immobility or economic stagnation. The notion of karma can indeed have social side-effects. In Japan, for example, it has been used to justify social discrimination against certain groups of individuals previously known as *eta* ("impure") and nowadays referred to as *burakumin* ("hamlet people"). Yet the notion of karmic retribution has made a broad contribution to moralizing life in society and encouraging individuals to improve their social standing. Karma leads to everything, even to Awakening – provided that one can put an end to it.

"Buddhism denies the existence of a self"

*Buddhism stands unique in the history of human thought in deny-
ing the existence of such a Soul, Self, or Ātman.*
Walpola Rahula, *What the Buddha Taught*, 1959

*The buddhas spoke of the self as well as teaching about the non-self.
They also taught that there is neither a self nor a non-self.*
Nāgārjuna, ca. third century

The denial of the self, ego, or of the individual soul (*anātman*) is
the touchstone or perhaps rather the stumbling block of the
Buddhist doctrine. This may appear to present a paradox, given
that this is a religion which claims to be based on individual salvation. In a special issue of *Le Nouvel Observateur* on Buddhism,
Frédéric Lenoir noted that "the vast majority of people involved
in Buddhism claim that it provides them with the means of developing their individual potential. The emergence of this subject is
an ultra-western idea."

Of all the dogmas of canonical Buddhism, *anātman* is undoubtedly the one which has been the greatest cause of debate as it seems
to go against common sense. The majority of commentators feel
that this dogma is the most striking indicator of the originality of
Buddhism compared to other religions. The significance and impact
of this doctrine should also be questioned by placing it in its original
context as well as the context of its subsequent development.

According to Buddhist scholasticism, the self is purely the result
of physical and mental processes, a sort of "mental fabrication"
which has no ultimate reality. Awakening involves becoming
aware of this illusory nature of the self. As the monk Nāgasena
(second century BC) put it in his famous apologue: "Just as, when
certain pieces of wood are assembled, we talk of a chariot; in the

49

same way, when the five physical and mental components are present, we talk of the 'Self'." These five groups or "aggregates" (*skandha*), are impermanent and therefore contribute to the impermanence of the self. They are: form (or matter, *rūpa*), sensations (*vedanā*), perceptions (*samjnā*), mental formations (*samskāra*), and consciousness (*vijñāna*).

The French philosopher Blaise Pascal sounded like a Buddhist when he said that the self is detestable or when he demonstrated the impossibility of locating this self in any particular part of the body. Today, in the light of recent scientific discoveries in neurology, we know that the self is merely the result of a group of mental or neurological structures and that a brain tumor or cell degeneration is enough to have a profound effect on this self. Similarly, psychoanalytical research into the subconscious mind has dealt a swift blow to the Cartesian notion of an independent and rational self. In this sense at least, Buddhist psychology appears to be compatible with the modern way of thinking. Nevertheless, the denial of the self does not have the same meaning in an individualist society like those of the West as in a traditional society like India's at the time of the Buddha, where the individual, according to our understanding of the word, was the exception and not the norm.

Taken back to its original Indian context, the Buddhist notion of *anātman* is the opposite of the Hindu belief in the existence of the *ātman* or self in each being and is perhaps, first and foremost, a claim to doctrinal originality, a kind of attempt to outdo the dominant religion. Actually, the Hindu *ātman*, a spark of the absolute or Brahman within each being, is different from the personal *ātman* denied by Buddhism. Living beings can perish but this divine core within them does not die. Instead it transmigrates from life to life before returning to its source.

How can we continue to say that Buddhism is a religion of individual salvation if the individual (or the self) does not exist? And if those bodhisattva-practitioners, while rejecting the dualist distinction between self and other, are committed to saving all beings before saving themselves?

The Buddhist position on this issue is therefore distinctly more complex than the dogma of the absence of self would seem to imply. Furthermore, the concept of self has to retain a slight element of reality if the notion of karmic retribution is to be retained, upon which the Buddhist moral doctrine is based. If, for example, there is no one there to pay for a broken pot, how do we dissuade someone from breaking it in the first place? The notions of the "self" (*ātman*) and person (*purusha*) therefore remain in use when it comes to the conventional truth even if they are denied, in principle, in the name of ultimate truth. No matter how often we hear that the self is empty, it remains no less real when it comes to beliefs and everyday practices.

By emphasizing questions of ethical responsibility, early Buddhism tended to favor the individuality of its followers. The very notion of responsibility implies that an individual is responsible for his actions. The self is, amongst other things, a juridical fiction, but is nevertheless a necessary fiction for life in society. Buddhist discipline as a whole, based on the notions of confession and repentance, can be seen as a method of attributing blame, i.e. of individualizing. This method appears, in practice, to deny the theory of *anātman* which, literally speaking, boils down to a denial of all individual responsibility or even a denial of all spiritual progress or deliverance. We therefore arrive at the paradox, expressed by the Mahāyāna, that there is a path but nobody who follows it.

The fact that the five physical and mental components of personality do not include a substantial or permanent self does not prevent us from seeking one outside of these components, beyond our ordinary consciousness. This is why Buddhist introspection sometimes defines itself as a search for the true self which is no longer the narrow ego but rather a superior reality, for example the buddha nature. The interest shown by various schools of the Mahāyāna in notions such as "pure mind" and "storehouse consciousness" is sometimes, and quite justifiably no doubt, denounced as a return to the belief in a notion of the same type as the Brahmanic *ātman*. But we must keep in mind that the subject in question is no longer the shallow ego, but rather the real self, the dreamer finally awoken from his long dream.

The emphasis the majority of scholars have placed on the orthodox dogma of the *anātman* again reflects an elitist or even ideological vision of Buddhism: in fact, it is clear that the majority of followers of mainstream Buddhism believe in the existence of a self and that their observance of the religion is based on this very belief. The so-called "orthodox" or rather monastic conception of the non-existence of the self fails to take account of the complexity of the Buddhist tradition and the diversity of its responses to the serious question of subjectivity.

— "Buddhism teaches reincarnation" —

Everything seems to indicate that your little Jesse is the reincarnation of the sacred lama Dorje ...
Gordon MacGill, *Little Buddha*, 1994

The question of the reincarnation of Tibetan lamas has long fascinated Westerners. It always forms a focal point in any discussion on the rational or irrational nature of Buddhism. This also explains the appeal of films like *Little Buddha*.

Bertolucci's film interweaves two stories: the story of the Buddha and that of a child living in Seattle with his parents at the end of the twentieth century whom two Tibetan monks in exile identify as the reincarnation of one of their eminent lamas. The viewer has the definite impression that the same protagonist is being reincarnated from one life to another, from ancient India through to modern-day America, just as if the Tibetan dogma of reincarnation were directly descended from the teachings of the Buddha.

It is, however, necessary to distinguish this Tibetan type of reincarnation from the Buddhist dogma of transmigration which is merely a consequence of the doctrine of karma. Transmigration is, in fact, the passing of any being from one life to another, at a level of existence determined by his or her karma, whereas Tibetan reincarnation implies the rebirth of a charismatic individual: certain beings can choose the form in which they wish to reappear to pursue their mission.

It takes an excessive shift in meaning to present this relatively late and purely Tibetan institution as stemming from orthodox Buddhism. In fact, the notion only developed at the end of the twelfth century in the Karmapa school when one of the great lamas of the school, Düsum Khyempa, had the idea of foretelling his own rebirth. This notion had the advantage of keeping the prestige of a charismatic master alive within the school after death. The idea spread like wildfire to the other schools, notably the Gelugpa, which used it to establish the lineage of the Dalai Lamas.

The phenomenon of reincarnation should therefore be viewed within its cultural context – that of the Tibetan culture. Until recently, it was in fact limited to Tibet and the surrounding kingdoms (Bhutan, Sikkim, Ladakh, Mongolia) and barely played any part in Indian Buddhism itself, nor in other Indianized or Sinicized forms of Buddhism which developed in Asia.

The geographical area which upholds this belief in reincarnation has extended gradually from Tibet towards Mongolia. Thus, when the third Dalai Lama died – the first to have been given the title of Mongol leader Altan Khan – his reincarnation, the fourth Dalai Lama, was discovered in Mongolia in the body of a child who, by some happy coincidence, turned out to be the great grandson of Altan Khan. More recently, following the exile of many Tibetans, it has started to spread to Europe and North America – as shown precisely by *Little Buddha*. As noted by the Tibetan lama Dagyab Rimpoche: "The number of lamas in exile has increased like an inflation!" However, no reincarnated lama has yet been found among Afro-Americans or Latinos, let alone among the communist Chinese. Without dwelling too much on the ethnic criteria for Awakening, the distinct political nature of certain reincarnations has undoubtedly called the validity of the institution into question. The media have reported on the rivalry between the Chinese and Tibetans concerning the reincarnation of the Panchen Lama (the other great spiritual authority of Tibetan Buddhism, along with the Dalai Lama) and that of the sixteenth Karmapa.

The matter becomes all the more complicated when it emerges that it is not just the lama as an individual who can be reincarnated into another person; the lama's body, his verbal principle, and his mind can also be reincarnated separately. This may or may not occur within the same lineage and may take place simultaneously or at different points in time.

The system of reincarnation has existed in Tibet for centuries and its benefits have rarely been questioned either by the Tibetans themselves or by Westerners. The Chinese too have not questioned these benefits and have managed to turn the charisma of certain lamas to their own advantage. The question remains to be asked what other Buddhists think of this system, since they evidently do not hold it in sufficiently high regard to make it an article of faith, despite its apparent advantages.

There is nothing new in political appropriation of this kind; indeed, it was the notion of reincarnation which enabled the Gelugpa school to seize the main monasteries of the other schools and allowed their leader, the fifth Dalai Lama, to become a sort of divine king of Tibet with the benediction of the Mongols. However, there are drawbacks to this system: ever since it came into existence, the succession of Dalai Lamas has been little more than a long series of intrigues in the monasteries or at the palace. During the period from the discovery of a new reincarnation to the maturity of the new Dalai Lama, the government was controlled by a regent who often sought to remain in power. Thus, during the eighteenth and nineteenth centuries, four Dalai Lamas died before ascending the throne, some in mysterious circumstances. Fortunately, this state of affairs ended with the thirteenth Dalai Lama.

The current Dalai Lama is more than just the reincarnation of his predecessor; he is also, in principle, one of the many manifestations of Avalokiteshvara, one of the great bodhisattvas of Mahāyāna and the mythical parent of the Tibetan race. When asked why Avalokiteshvara had chosen to appear in masculine form in Tibet, thereby forgoing a chance to promote the feminine cause, the Dalai Lama replied that this was to avoid clashing with Tibetan prejudices relating to male supremacy. This response is somewhat surprising, given that some of the other great divinities of Tibetan Buddhism are feminine (such as Tārā) and that in China and Japan – two countries not exactly renowned for their feminism – this same bodhisattva (known as Guanyin in Chinese and Kannon in Japanese) appears in feminine form.

Perhaps this system has now served its time. In an age when Chinese communists are actively seeking to find reincarnated lamas among their supporters, for the Tibetans the disadvantages are beginning to outweigh the advantages. The present Dalai Lama's declaration that he would not be reincarnated is perhaps best interpreted within this context.

The system of reincarnation has also played an important part in the history of Bhutan, a royal kingdom which borders Tibet. Bhutan became an independent political unit in the seventeenth century thanks to Ngawang Namgyel, a Tibetan monk who took refuge here when the prince of Tsang refused to recognize him as the legitimate reincarnation of a master of the Drukpa sect. As head of the Bhutanese Drukpa, he imposed himself as the first sovereign (*shabdrung*) of Bhutan, having resisted attacks by Tibet. Legend has it that, when he died in 1705, three rays of light left his body corresponding to three lines of reincarnation: that of his body, his verbal principle, and his mind. These multiple lines of reincarnation led to ongoing quarrels about succession. The body line quickly died out. That of the verbal principle died out in 1918. The mind line, the most noble of all, successfully asserted itself in 1734, allowing a certain degree of political stability. It died out with the death of the sixth and last *shabdrung* in 1931.

Part II
Buddhism and Local Cultures

"Buddhism is an atheistic religion"

[The Buddha] took great pride in being human and in being no more than this. In fact, he degraded the gods, placing them beneath mankind on the scale of living beings.

Giuseppe Tucci, in *Présence du Bouddhisme*, 1987

Buddhism, it is often said, has no use for God, let alone gods. Certainly early Buddhism did not recognize a creator god or demiurge like Hinduism or the monotheistic religions of the West. According to Buddhism, the universe is regulated by an impersonal law – the Dharma. However, the situation changed with the development of the Mahāyāna school: the numerous buddhas and bodhisattvas constituted a real pantheon of divinities, all with different virtues and functions. If we take this idea a step further: with the cosmic Buddha Mahavairochana (whose name signifies Great Sun), defined as the sovereign principle of all things, we are not far from the concept of a personal God. Similarly, in the Pure Land school, the buddha Amitābha (better known under his Japanese name of Amida) is generally regarded as a savior: he does, after all, promise that he will guide all those who invoke him to his Pure Land in the west, a sort of Buddhist paradise from where they can no longer fall back down to the lower world.

As noted by the French scholar André Bareau: "As the sons of India, the Buddha and his disciples shared all the ideas of their compatriots … on the existence of numerous gods and spirits populating heaven and earth" (*Le Bouddhisme indien*, 1966). And yet Matthieu Ricard, in *The Monk and the Philosopher*, argues that Buddhism is not a polytheism, and that the representations of divinities in Tibetan religion have nothing to do with "gods" as entities leading some kind of autonomous existence. Instead, they are "archetypes of knowledge, of compassion, of altruism, etc., which are objects of meditation and bring out these qualities in us through visualization techniques." This viewpoint, however, is only representative of an intellectual (and often Westernized) elite. The Dalai Lama himself has declared that he makes all his important decisions based on oracles delivered by his own personal soothsayer during trances whereby the latter is possessed by one of these fearsome deities of Tibetan Buddhism.

While, in theory, these deities are declared to be symbolic, in practice they are taken very seriously. Tibetan Buddhists could say of their gods and demons what the marquise du Deffand, on the eve of the French Revolution, said of ghosts: "I don't believe in them, but I'm scared of them." Clearly this is not something which Buddhist lamas boast about to their Western disciples as they are very aware that these Westerners, raised in a culture of rationalism, are somewhat scornful of what they would deem to be "superstition."

This same double language can be found in Japanese Buddhism. The Sōtō Zen master Keizan Jōkin (1268–1325), for example, stated to anyone who would listen that a Zen patriarch obeys "neither a god – let alone God – nor a master," while at the same time claiming that he often had visions of deities in his dreams and that he followed their recommendations to the letter. Keizan is not an isolated case; indeed, he is highly representative of medieval Japanese monks on this point.

Japanese Buddhism makes the distinction between purely "symbolic" gods (which are known as "temporary manifestations" or *gongen*) and "real" gods or demons. While the former are merely hypostases of the higher principle, the latter cannot be so easily reduced to abstractions. They persist in their evil ways, and monks sometimes have to "liberate" them ritually (a euphemism which refers to ritual murder) to bring them to order. In the best-case scenario, they subjugate or convert them, transforming them into "protectors" of Buddhism.

Tibetan Buddhism too recognizes the distance between symbol and reality in distinguishing between *yidam*, elective deities chosen by the follower who visualizes them during practice and *chökyong* or "protectors," threatening deities who, once placated by the practitioner, protect him or her against the forces of evil.

While some see the "historical" Buddha as simply the founder of a resolutely atheist Buddhism, for the majority of Buddhists he is the most eminent character in a vast cosmopolitan pantheon and as such is an important object of worship. Is Buddhism therefore atheist, monotheist, or even polytheist? Let's investigate this issue more closely.

The gods were the first inhabitants of the Buddhist cosmos – its rulers – before being evicted and then in certain cases reinstated (at a subordinate level) by the Buddha and his retinue. According to orthodoxy, even if Buddhism does recognize the existence of native gods, they differ from the Buddha and the Buddhist saints in that they are subject to the law of cause and effect. Their divine status is the result of good karma and is only temporary. They may acquire superhuman powers for a time but they are in no way completely free and all-powerful beings, as is believed by Hindus for example. They are also at a disadvantage compared to humans as they are so busy enjoying a life of divine bliss, which they believe to be eternal, that they become neglectful of karmic reality and forget to practice the Buddhist law which could save them.

Furthermore, in Mahāyāna, the gods eventually lost (at least in theory) what little reality and independence they still had: they become simple projections of the human mind, illusions caused by our karma, or abstract entities created by our mind. They are also often perceived to be local and culturally determined manifestations of the various buddhas and bodhisattvas. In practice, however, most Buddhists still believe in them without question.

In general, the further a god climbs in the celestial hierarchy, the fewer direct links he has with humans. Of course, there are significant exceptions to this such as certain great bodhisattvas who are both perfect and near. However, because the lesser gods are subject to the law of causality, like us, they prove to be more accessible: they benefit from rituals carried out for them and in return protect people. They can also benefit from the teachings of Buddhist masters, thereby achieving Awakening.

So who are these Buddhist gods? Paradoxically, it could be said that the Buddha himself ranks highest among them. Without wishing to attribute too much credibility to the Hindu (and therefore somewhat polemical) theory which states that the Buddha himself is merely the ninth avatar (reincarnation) of the great God Vishnu, it cannot be denied that various aspects of the image of the Buddha have been inherited from the image of the Hindu gods. The seven steps taken by the Buddha as a child just after his birth to take possession of the universe are for example reminiscent of the three steps taken by one of Vishnu's avatars to conquer the Triple World. According to the Japanese master Nichiren (1222–82), "Shākyamuni [the Buddha] is the lord, the mother and father, the original master of all the beings of this world."

Endowed with the thirty-two marks of the buddhas, Shākyamuni is indeed treated as a kind of god. Mahāyāna scriptures such as the *Lotus Sutra* depict him as an eternal, all-knowing, and transcendent being whose human vulnerability is simply a pious stratagem. This notion of a supra-worldly Buddha gave rise to a whole series of metaphysical buddhas such as Amitābha (the buddha who reigns over the Western Pure Land) and the five *dhyāni* buddhas who correspond to the five directions of the *mandala* (four buddhas at the four cardinal points with Shākyamuni at the center, later replaced by Vairochana). In esoteric Buddhism in particular, the cosmic Buddha Vairochana, likened to the sun, is perceived as the be-all and end-all of all things.

After the buddhas come the bodhisattvas, considered to be either future buddhas or emanations of the various buddhas. The former case is represented by Maitreya, the "future Buddha," who is said to wait in Tushita heaven until it is time (far away for us but close for him) to appear in our world, in several million years' time. Unlike the Christian Messiah, however, Maitreya will not appear at the end of the world; instead he will mark the start of the new golden age after our world has completely renewed itself.

Without a doubt, the most popular bodhisattva is Avalokiteshvara (Guanyin in Chinese, Kannon in Japanese), the bodhisattva of compassion often represented as having feminine and even maternal traits. Certain texts claim that Avalokiteshvara is simply a manifestation of the Buddha Amitābha, although in popular faith he/she has acquired a separate personality. Another bodhisattva of particular importance in China and Japan is Kshitigarbha (Dizang in Chinese, Jizō in Japanese), represented as an amiable young monk. In popular Buddhism, he guides the "souls" of the dead at the crossroads of the six "paths" and intercedes on their behalf with the infernal judges. As a result, he has come to be known more particularly as the protector of dead children.

Other purely Buddhist "deities" include the *arhats* (*luohan* in Chinese, *rakan* in Japanese). These disciples of the "historical" Buddha have become extraordinary people in Sino-Japanese Buddhism, resembling Taoist immortals in certain respects. They are venerated collectively by Buddhists in the form of sixteen, eighteen, or 500 *arhats*. The latter were first introduced to a Western audience by the Jesuit missionary Matteo Ricci, who encountered their representations shortly after his arrival in China. Ironically, Ricci himself was subsequently deified among these 500 *arhats*. Although the majority of these *arhats* are not worshiped as individuals, one of them became an important object of worship: Pindola (Binzuru in Japanese), sometimes called the "wandering Jew" of Buddhism.

Then come a number of Indian, Chinese, and Japanese deities acquired by Buddhism after adapting to new cultures encountered on the way. These include Indra and Brahmā, two major gods of the Indian pantheon who evolved to become protectors of Buddhism. By contrast, the other great Indian gods, most notably Shiva and Vishnu, are passed over in silence. While the conversion of local gods to the new religion has been mostly smooth, in certain cases it requires a submission, involving a degree of symbolic violence. The method of these conversions reflects the relationship of Buddhism with local religion. Hinduism and Buddhism have long been rival religions, and in Hindu mythology the Buddha is reduced to being a simple avatar of Vishnu who appeared only to trick the heretics (meaning Buddhists) and lead them to ruin.

The image of Shiva in sexual union with his consort (symbolizing his creative energy) considerably influenced representations in later Buddhism, notably in its Tantric form. Shiva's son, the elephant-headed god Ganesha, appears in the form of a double and ambivalent god in Japanese esotericism, and is both good and evil. He is represented by two male and female deities, with human bodies and the head of an elephant, standing in sexual embrace. This dual-bodied deity, also called "Deity of Bliss" (Kangiten), has never been recognized as completely orthodox, yet enjoyed considerable occult influence in medieval Japan.

It could therefore be said that two types of belief coexist in Buddhism. The first sees gods as a category of beings linked to desire who owe their temporary success to a good karma. They have none of the supreme powers which Hinduism and other religions attribute to them and, like everyone else, are subject to the laws of desire, suffering, and karmic retribution. They can only expect to achieve salvation through converting to Buddhism, which they must vow to protect.

The doctrine of emptiness featured in Mahāyāna states that the gods only exist at the level of conventional truth. When it comes to the ultimate truth they, like all things, are empty and unreal. The Buddha is the only real being because he is emptiness itself. The more knowledgeable followers see the gods as merely convenient instruments of teaching, white lies that should not be taken too seriously. In Tantric Buddhism, the gods – projections of various spiritual faculties – must initially be visualized to then be mentally dissolved.

Yet there are cases, albeit rare, of monks not being able to outdo powerful local deities or stubborn demons, despite the arsenal of rituals and spiritual "powers" they have acquired through their ascetic and contemplative practice. Such deities and demons are often one and the same: certain local deities are turned into demons by Buddhists when they refuse to convert, whereas certain demons become deities when they accept the Buddhist precepts, either grudgingly or by force. Certain legends show how, in some rare cases, Buddhism has to admit defeat. The myth of Gozu Tennō (the bull-headed heavenly king), a Japanese god or demon of epidemics, is particularly significant in this respect. After taking vengeance on a lay disciple of the Buddha who refused him hospitality, this deity took on the Buddha himself whom he ended up killing by infecting him. This story was told by Yin-Yang masters, rivals to Buddhism, around the fourteenth century during the era when nascent Shintō was beginning to regain the ground abandoned by the Japanese gods, and demonstrates that Buddhists could not simply ignore these gods or treat them with scorn.

Buddhism could be described as a polytheistic religion in the sense that it recognizes the relative existence of numerous gods who act as mediators or even saviors, becoming objects of worship. However, given that the ultimate reality is that of the Buddha, Buddhism could also be described as monotheistic. Finally, given that this Buddha is not a god in the Western sense of the term and is considered to be either the first to have understood this ultimate reality (according to early Buddhism) or another name for this ultimate reality (according to Mahāyāna), Buddhism could also, at a pinch, be described as atheistic. Clearly these rigid categories are not appropriate for describing this complex phenomenon and its fluid beliefs and practices.

—————— "Buddhism is above all —————— a spirituality"

Buddhism is a religion of interiority.

Le Nouvel Observateur, 2003

The vision of Buddhism as a spirituality is undoubtedly what makes it so attractive to us in today's world. The notion of spirituality seems to meet the needs of many Westerners who no longer identify with the religion of their parents yet do not adhere to a purely materialistic vision of the world. This notion implies a certain criticism of ritualism, which they perceive to be something of an empty shell. Although Western cultures primarily subscribe to the Christian tradition, a certain degree of criticism of Buddhist tradition is also evident which is not unlike the Protestant criticism of Catholic ritual (Luther saw the Mass as a form of magic). Those attracted to Buddhism through a growing dislike for what they perceive to be outdated rituals in Christianity and Judaism have adopted the Protestant criticism of ritualism, without even knowing the latter in some cases, as it became part of the zeitgeist.

Paradoxically, ritual often lives on as a phenomenon of identification among certain Western followers of Buddhism insofar as it identifies their adherence to a non-Western religion. Certain followers recite Japanese or Tibetan prayers, for example, without understanding a word, which they would undoubtedly refuse to do if it were a matter of reciting Latin in church. While they do sometimes attempt to translate these prayers to preserve at least the sense if not the form (if the two are indeed dissociable), this becomes difficult when the recitation contains elements which appear to be devoid of sense, such as the mantras.

For the vast majority of its Asian followers, however, Buddhism is first and foremost a form of ritual, and its rituals are apotropaic (destined to ward off evil) or magical (aiming to procure worldly benefits such as success, health, prestige, or wealth). This is certainly the case when it comes to the veneration of the Buddha's relics, a form of worship which reminded Victor Segalen of the most questionable aspects of Catholicism.

In a section of his *Journal des Îles,* which was written during his journey to Ceylon (Sri Lanka) in 1904 Segalen, outraged by the devotion of the Singhalese to the relic of the Buddha's tooth, noted: "I have fallen back down from the master, and it really is a fall, down to worship, to the manifestations of the populace, to relics." And he concludes: "From now on, I will vigorously separate the undefined conglomerate of myths, cycles, counting of years, of the numerous fleeting Buddhas, from everything which obstructs and crushes the work of the Master. It's a real shame that there is only one word: *Buddhism* to signify these varieties and that this word itself is comical, stocky, bulbous, paunchy and beatific. From now on I will say to myself: the Teachings of Siddharta: the man-who-attained-his-goal."

This common dichotomy between the "original" Buddhism and popular "superstition" in the name of a pure ideal is offensive to the living reality of Buddhism. Buddhism does not and has never existed beyond those who practice it and, in historical reality, these forms of worship that seem to us to be based on "superstition" all stem as much from the clerical elite as from the populace. Furthermore, such forms of worship are not usually "white lies" or a "betrayal of the clerics" with the aim of calming simple souls. People do not bow down before statues of the buddhas and other gods all their life long without seeing them as something more than just symbols or allegories.

The magical aspect of Buddhism has unfortunately been completely neglected in the West to date, which has focused instead on its spiritual or doctrinal aspects. "Supranormal powers" (*abhijña*), allegedly obtained through asceticism or ritual, are contrasted with pure spirituality. Even though these powers have never been the avowed goal of religious observance in Asia, they particularly appeal to the imagination of followers who count on the clergy to protect them from all evil and guarantee them happiness in this world and the next.

By depicting the Buddha as a kind of freethinker rising up against the prejudices of his time, the Orientalists of the nineteenth century transformed Buddhism into a kind of "Protestantism" characterized by its rejection of dogma and ritual. They found in Buddhism a religion after their own heart whose supposedly rationalist approach formed an enlightening contrast with Christianity (in particular ritualistic Catholicism). This same attitude can be found among the Western Buddhist elite who are seeking, in good faith, to reform Buddhism and transform it into a religion which is adapted to the modern world. In doing so, they are forgetting one thing: Buddhist philosophy, metaphysics, myth, and ritual form an organic whole; it is impossible to dispense with one (ritual) without distorting the others. In the living reality of Buddhism, the philosophical and the religious, the rational and the magic, go hand in hand.

This anti-ritual interpretation of Buddhism is particularly evident in a number of recent books about Buddhism. In *The Monk and the Philosopher*, for instance, Matthieu Ricard declares: "Deities are symbolic. The face of a deity represents the One, the absolute. Its two arms are the knowledge of Emptiness united to the method of Compassion. Certain deities have six arms that symbolize the six perfections ... These symbolic archetypes enable us to use the power of our imagination as a factor of spiritual progress instead of letting ourselves be swept along by unrestrained thoughts." As a result, "prostration before the Buddha is a respectful homage, not to a god but to he who incarnates the ultimate wisdom."

When it comes to funerary rituals, which are very important in all forms of Buddhism – especially Japanese Buddhism – we are told that these rituals are also purely symbolic. Tell that to the relatives of the deceased who often pay a very high price to ensure the salvation of their loved one as well as, in certain cases, to dispose of the deceased in accordance with regulations, so that he or she does not return to haunt the living.

The individualized character of Buddhism is also often emphasized (meditation is the internal and therefore solitary activity par excellence). However, this religion also has a marked communal aspect: the *sangha* or community is the third refuge for followers alongside the Dharma and the Buddha. Even behaviors which seem highly individualized to us, such as contemplative practice, are socially determined in their Asian context. This is sure to bring displeasure to those who have turned to Buddhism in search of an internal and intensely personal experience. It results in some doubt being cast on the "third refuge" and questions whether the Buddha really imposed the idea of the community or if this was merely a simple stop-gap solution for the fallible.

This denial of the collective and ritual dimensions of Buddhism shows that an idealized Buddhism can obscure the most obvious sociological realities. Indeed, anyone who has observed life in a Buddhist monastery without prejudice will know that rituals form an important part of everyday activities, to the detriment of contemplation per se. But sometimes even monks have an idealized view of their practice, and tend to downplay ritual as purely symbolic. In Ricard's view, for instance, "a *stūpa* (funeral mound) is a symbol of the spirit of Buddha. The scriptures symbolize his words and the statues his body." Similarly, the magical aspect of mantra is overlooked so that only its etymological sense is retained: namely "that which protects the spirit," not from a calamity as such but rather from distraction or mental confusion. The problem is that this etymology is practically unheard of, or plays a marginal role, for the majority of ordinary Buddhists.

A similar denial is reflected in Ricard's notion that the prayer wheels of Tibetan Buddhism, far from being a convenient substitute for reciting prayers, are an external support, enabling believers to link to an internal truth. Canonical sources are, of course, full of symbolical and allegorical interpretations. Nevertheless the fact remains that interpretations of this kind are merely rationalizations for the majority of Asian followers, with no relation to their everyday lives. It is undoubtedly the Western conception of Buddhist *stūpas*, icons, prayer wheels – and symbols in general – as expressed here that needs to be reviewed.

Too often, the denial of the practical function of Buddhist objects and the emphasis on their symbolic or aesthetic value is a way to assert the "spiritual" nature of the Buddhist experience. This interpretation, however, reflects only the views of an elitist minority of Asian and Western practitioners. While the practice of Buddhism aims in principle to transcend any socio-cultural conditioning, it is not simply a "pure experience." To see Buddhism as pure spirituality, a realization of oneself with libertarian undertones, is to overlook its disciplinarian aspect as expressed in the vast canonical literature of Vinaya. Buddhism is both an internal experience and a social structure at the same time.

The reinterpretation of Buddhism as "spirituality" is particularly striking in the case of Zen. In *Zen and the Birds of Appetite*, the Catholic monk Thomas Merton writes: "To define Zen in terms of a religious system or structure is in fact to destroy it – or rather to miss it completely." He adds that "very serious and qualified" practitioners of Zen deny that it is a religion, citing as his authorities Dōgen – a sect founder who was renowned for his sectarian polemics – and D. T. Suzuki, a renowned ideologist. According to Merton: "Buddhism itself … points beyond any theological or philosophical 'ism.' It *insists on not being a system* (while at the same time, like other religions, presenting a peculiar temptation to systematizers)." Merton is correct to stress that this demand not to be a system is shared by most religious systems: their very legitimacy is based on this point – making it somewhat suspect.

Numerous Western followers of Buddhism share this emphasis on personal experience to the detriment of the doctrine and the system. However, somewhat paradoxically, their discourse tends to hide behind generic doctrinal descriptions rather than relating to their own experiences. Without denying the reality of these experiences, one should note that those who claim to have them rarely move away from the realm of belief – a belief which, in principle, is not all that different from the "superstitions" adhered to by the less advanced practitioners which they are endeavoring to denigrate.

—— "The Dalai Lama is the spiritual —— leader of Buddhism"

We are all your most faithful servants, O Great Lama, give, direct your light on us!
Antonin Artaud, "Address to the Dalai Lama", 1925

The vogue of Tibetan Buddhism in Europe and the United States is primarily due to the undeniable charisma – reinforced by intense media coverage – of the current Dalai Lama, Tenzin Gyatso, the fourteenth holder of the title. However, although Tibetan Buddhism accounts for two-thirds of cases of conversion in Europe and the United States, it represents only 2 percent of Buddhists in Asia. For many, the Dalai Lama, whose name means "Ocean of Wisdom," is the incarnation of Buddhist compassion and tolerance. His institutional role, however, is relatively limited: he is by no means the "Pope of the Buddhist church" (as he was still called not so long ago in the West). Even though he has come to personify Tibetan nationalism, he is, technically speaking, only the spiritual chief of the Tibetan Buddhist communities in Tibet and in exile.

The idealization of the Dalai Lama is primarily the result of an idealization of traditional Tibet and of Tibetan Buddhism. The myth of Shangri-La (a Buddhist paradise in the Himalayas), for example, identifies Tibet as the spiritual high point of the world – and, by contrast, the occupation of that country by Chinese troops took on the meaning of a drama where the spiritual destiny of the world is at stake. The myth became famous after the 1937 film *Lost Horizon* by Frank Capra (based on the novel by James Hilton), but the underlying idea dates back much further than this.

Tibet's capital city Lhasa remained closed to outsiders throughout most of the nineteenth century, fueling the imagination of the Western world. When Francis Younghusband led the British troops into the city in 1904, he sent the following telegram to the Swedish explorer Sven Hedin, who had spent a long time camping outside the city, without being allowed to enter: "Sorry, I have deflowered the city of your dreams." Despite the fact that a more mundane and military reality has infiltrated the Tibetan dream, the travel tales of explorer Alexandra David-Néel as well as publications by the alleged lama Lobsang Rampa – who is now known to have been a British charlatan – have continued to add credibility to the idea of a "spiritual" Tibet. The idea has also established itself in popular culture thanks to the influence of various media such as the famous comic strip *Tintin in Tibet* – so much so that, for some Western intellectuals, any Tibetan nomad becomes a living buddha.

For those who think that all Tibetan monks are paragons of virtue, the autobiography of the monk Tashi Khedrup provides a more sober version of the reality and rectifies any clichés about the spiritual motivations of monks and life in a monastery. Like many of his fellow monks, Tashi Khedrup entered the order without any religious calling whatsoever. In fact, he was something of a bully who quickly found his role in the monastery as a monk policeman (*dob-dob*). His unostentatious tales often have more to do with his brawls than with his spiritual experiences.

Paradoxically, despite being spokesman for a very ancient tradition, the Dalai Lama has brought an air of modernity to Tibetan Buddhism. His speeches and writings focus on the similarities between Buddhism and science and reveal a great interest in recent scientific discoveries. He also makes constant reference to tolerance, compassion, respect for life, and human and universal responsibility. He has even gone so far as to declare that, if he returned to power, he would make Tibet a demilitarized zone, a sort of ecological and spiritual reserve for mankind. It is for all of these reasons that he was awarded the Nobel Peace Prize in 1989, the same year the Berlin Wall came down. Through him (Tibetan) Buddhism has been perceived as a sort of spiritual humanism specially adapted to the new ethical problems raised by the "humanitarian" crisis and by modern scientific progress. In fact, these are more the values of an alterglobalist counter-culture than of traditional Buddhism.

The Dalai Lama represents a Buddhism that is more representative of Tibetans in exile and their Western followers than of Tibetans in Tibet. Furthermore, in their denial of anything Chinese, Tibetans in exile and their Western supporters have tended to downplay the crucial role of mediator played in Beijing by the Panchen Lama (this superior of the Tibetan monastery of Tashilumpo was once revered as highly as the Dalai Lama) until his death in 1989. The Dalai Lama himself is not, in theory, the spiritual chief of any school in particular and maintains good relations with them all. However, the fact that he is part of the Gelugpa school explains why his supporters continue to favor this school, which has dominated the political and religious scene since the fifth Dalai Lama came to power in 1642.

Furthermore, when we talk of Tibetan religion, we tend to overlook the other great religious tradition of Tibet, the Bön tradition. Actually, the current Bön tradition, which claims to date back to the pre-Buddhist "nameless religion" of Tibet, seems to have formed relatively late, around the eleventh century, and has apparently been strongly influenced by Buddhism (it shares in particular many features with the Nyingmapa school and places a great deal of importance on local deities).

As French Tibetologist Anne-Marie Blondeau notes, writing on "Religions du Tibet," in *Histoire des Religions*: "The speeches and writings of the Dalai Lama and his entourage seem to indicate a desire for the transformation or adaptation of Tibetan Buddhism to place it within the framework of a universal Buddhism ... The result is a certain reluctance to let outsiders show any deeper interest in the heterodox religious traditions. If this trend continues, Tibetan Buddhism could lose the profoundly original character that makes its valuable."

Despite his spirit of tolerance, the Dalai Lama has not always been able to prevent internecine fights between the various groups which make up the community of Tibetans in exile. One particularly significant case deserves a mention here. This involves the worship of a Tantric deity by the name of Dorje Shugden, the reincarnation of a deceased lama who used to be the rival of the fifth Dalai Lama and was apparently assassinated by the latter's followers. In a strange twist, this deity went on to become the protector of the Gelugpa school and in particular of the current Dalai Lama, until he forbade his disciples from worshiping Shugden after receiving oracles from another of his protecting deities. This decision caused a general outcry among the followers of Shugden, who accused the Dalai Lama of being biased. The story was brought to the fore following the murder of a supporter of the Dalai Lama a few years ago. Aside from the issues relating to people and political dissension, this case serves to highlight the often strained relations between the various schools of Tibetan Buddhism and between the latter and local cults that were deemed to be unorthodox.

The Dalai Lama on Non-Violence

The principle of non-violence relating to the ultimate truth finds its limits in the world of conventional truth. At the start of the Iraq war, for example, the Dalai Lama stated: "In principle, any resort to violence is wrong. With regard to the Afghanistan and Iraq cases, only history will tell. At this moment, Afghanistan may be showing some positive results, but it is still not very stable. With Iraq, it is too early to say."

In another interview given at Boston's Fleet Center in October 2003, when asked about his opinion on the American invasion of Iraq, the Dalai Lama again responded with: "It is too early to say what will happen. Wait a few years. That is my opinion." Despite having publicly declared in the run-up to the war that wars create more problems than they resolve, once the hostilities had begun, he continued to reaffirm his confidence in "his friend" George Bush.

Clearly, the Dalai Lama is establishing a casuist distinction between the principle of violence and the political reality that may require a certain dose (substantial, in these cases) of violence. He goes a step further and redefines non-violence in a rather paradoxical manner. Speaking before the war, he said: "If one's motivation is sincere and positive but the circumstances require harsh behavior, essentially one is practicing non-violence" and "No matter what the case may be, I feel that a compassionate concern for the benefit of others – not simply for oneself – is the sole justification for the use of force." But who are these "others" in this case: allies or enemies? At any rate, he seems not to assign any great importance to the principle in the light of political reality. Yet he did stick to the principle in the case of Tibet. Truth on one side of the Pyrenees (or the Himalayas) and error on the other perhaps?

There may well be tactical reasons why he would opt to sit on the fence in this way, and in other contexts he clearly expressed his sympathy for Iraqis and his dismay at the loss of life. Still, in a situation of this kind, any form of neutrality between good and evil seems to be impossible – and the Middle Way itself appears somewhat suspect. As many have pointed out, not speaking out against this war from the outset boils down to political alignment with the United States. What would the Dalai Lama say to a religious leader asking for his opinion on the Chinese occupation of Tibet and repression of the Tibetan monks – "Wait a few years"?

Given the place the Dalai Lama holds in the world's imagination as an emblem of peace, it is disappointing that he would not condemn preemptive war outright, even at the risk of offending his allies in the United States government. His hesitation in doing so has attracted severe criticism, as expressed by historian Howard Zinn, in an interview on October 6, 2005: "I've always admired the Dalai Lama for his advocacy of nonviolence and his support of the rights of Tibet against Chinese domination ... But I must say I was disappointed to read his comment on the war in Iraq (i.e., 'Wait a few years'), because this is such an obvious, clear-cut moral issue in which massive violence has been used against Iraqis with many thousands of dead." Zinn goes on to add: "I wonder if the Dalai Lama knows enough about the history of US foreign policy. If he did, he would understand the real motives of our invasion of Iraq and would not be ambivalent about the present war and occupation" (cited in *The Progressive*, January 2006).

The confused rhetoric employed by the Dalai Lama is reminiscent of that used by some of his predecessors who supported the political powers and wished to wash their hands of any injustices committed by these powers. Good sentiment alone is not enough – a clear stance must be taken. Non-violence, in this case, seems to equate to a failure to act. In the recent upheaval of Tibet, many Tibetans seem to have reached this conclusion, even though they still claim to respect the Dalai Lama's authority.

—— "To be Buddhist is to be Zen" ——

Zen, along with Tibetan Buddhism, is one of the best known (or rather most misunderstood) forms of Buddhism in the West. For the majority of Western followers, Buddhism is an inner pathway, centered on meditation. According to Alexandra David-Néel "if you don't meditate, you have no real right to call yourself a Buddhist." The image which has established itself through Buddhist art is that of the Buddha sitting in meditation, and in fact this sitting and meditating (known in Japanese as *zazen*) has always constituted an essential part of Chinese Chan and its various Korean (Son), Vietnamese (Thien), and Japanese (Zen) forms.

The term Zen is derived from the Sanskrit *dhyāna* (pronounced *chan-na* in Chinese, hence the abbreviation *chan*, read *zen* in Japanese) which refers to meditation or, more specifically, concentration. Chan (the Chinese term for Zen) seems to have developed in China during the sixth century CE. At the beginning of the eighth century, the Chan movement split into two trends known as the Northern and Southern schools. The latter, which went on to become the orthodox form of Zen, advocated "sudden" Awakening and criticized its rival's alleged "gradualism" and, more specifically, its quietist or contemplative tendencies.

In the Tiantai sect (Tendai in Japanese), sitting meditation was just one of four forms of meditation or *samādhi*: (1) sitting-only *samādhi*; (2) walking-only *samādhi*; (3) half-sitting and half-walking *samādhi*; (4) "free form" *samādhi*. The second and third forms correspond to the "invocation of the Buddha Amida" as practiced most notably by the Pure Land schools. The fourth is the highest form and represents a kind of "active" meditation that consists of meditating during everyday activities. Manual labor, for example, is an important form of meditation in Zen, a trait which differentiates this school from other schools of Buddhism.

Traditional contemplation is only recommended in Chan as a method for beginners. While some see it as the supreme route of religious observance, seated meditation can also present a stumbling block. During the ninth century, the founder of the Linji sect (Rinzai in Japanese), Linji Yixuan, attacked the contemplative trend in no uncertain terms: "There are a bunch of blind baldheads who, having stuffed themselves with rice, sit doing Chan-style meditation practice, trying to arrest the flow of thoughts and stop them from arising, hating clamor, demanding silence – but these aren't Buddhist ways!" During another collective instruction, sensing, it seems, that his disciples were spending too much time in seated meditation, he declared: "Followers of the Way, when I say that there is no Law to be sought outside, apprentices do not understand me and immediately start looking inside, sitting by the wall in meditation, pressing their tongues against the roof of their mouths, absolutely still, never moving, supposing this to be the Dharma of the buddhas taught by the patriarchs. What a mistake!" And Linji went on to conclude: "In my view, the Dharma of the buddhas calls for no special undertakings. Just act ordinary, without trying to do anything particular. Move your bowels, piss, get dressed, eat your rice, and if you get tired, then lie down" (*The Record of Lin-chi*, translated by Ruth Fuller Sasaki).

We should not let ourselves be misled by Linji's diatribe: despite his disparagement, the act of sitting in meditation continued to play a significant role in the life of Zen monks, especially in the Japanese Sōtō sect. In the Rinzai sect, while it was not abandoned as such, this act of meditation was nevertheless challenged using the *kōan* method, a kind of riddle which puts a stop to discursive thought and where the solution to the puzzle is said to result in Awakening. In the thirteenth century, supporters of this sect criticized the "silent illumination Zen" (*mokushō zen*) which they considered to prove the quietism of the rival Sōtō sect.

The founder of the Sōtō sect, Dōgen, transformed the practice of *zazen* (which he referred to as *shikan taza* or "sitting only") into a sort of absolute that has come a long way from Indian *dhyāna*. It is no longer about introspection, but is instead a kind of ritual imitation of the emblematic posture of the buddhas. Followers sit and meditate not to achieve Awakening, but because this is exactly what the buddhas do. By adopting this sitting posture, they share momentarily in the state of buddha.

In Japan today, seated meditation is only practiced in a few large monasteries. In most Zen temples, as in the temples of other sects, priests spend most of their time carrying out funeral rituals for their parishioners. With the spread of Zen Buddhism throughout Europe and the United States, there has been a trend towards ignoring the more religious and ritualistic aspects of Zen and focusing instead on its technical aspects, thereby subjecting *zazen* to the same treatment as Indian yoga.

D. T. Suzuki and Zen

The spread of Zen in the West is owed in large part to D. T. Suzuki, whose *Essays in Zen Buddhism* exerted a significant influence on the 1960s and its hippy counter-culture as well as fascinating the previous generation. Such was the renown of Suzuki that he was even nick-named the "St. François Xavier of Zen for the Western world." Quite a fair turn of events, given that the missionary François Xavier sought to convert the Japanese in the sixteenth century.

Suzuki managed to convince his Western readers that Zen could rival the very best of Christian mysticism, or rather that it was, in fact, superior to all other forms of mysticism, both Oriental and Western, and as such constituted a unique historical phenomenon. Suzuki logically concluded that Zen is neither a philosophy nor a religion but is quite simply "the spirit of all religion or philosophy." It is precisely for this reason that Zen can be practiced by anyone, whether Buddhist or Christian, "just as big fish and small fish are both contentedly living in the same ocean." Through this metaphor, Zen is compared to the ocean while practicing Zen brings about what Romain Rolland called the "oceanic feeling" – the impression of fading away into the vast expanse of reality. The founder of psychoanalysis, Sigmund Freud, saw this notion of oceanic feeling as a form of primary narcissism. Suzuki, on the other hand, has had a significant impact upon the psychoanalytical reinterpretation of Zen by translating "no-mind" or "no-thought" (*wuxin* in Chinese, *mushin* in Japanese) – the aim of Zen meditation – as "Unconscious." By so doing, he deprived Zen of its religious nature and transformed it into a kind of therapeutic system. As we have seen, this same kind of misinterpretation has occurred in the case of Buddhism in general.

After stressing the universal nature of Zen, Suzuki then went on to emphasize the fact that this movement of Chinese origin could only develop to the full through contact with Japanese culture, seemingly without any fear of contradicting himself. In another of his works, entitled *Zen and Japanese Culture*, which was also extremely influential in Europe and the United States, he contrasted the purely intuitive nature of Zen with the cumbersome rationality of the West, establishing (in 1945!) the superiority of the sophisticated Japanese culture over the philistine culture of the West. Neglecting to comment on the responsibility of the Japanese in the development of the Pacific war, Suzuki saw the Hiroshima and Nagasaki bombings as a consequence of Western intellectualism: "The intellect presses the button and the entire city is destroyed." It apparently didn't occur to him to seek the main cause of the war and the destruction which followed in the same warrior mystique which he praises throughout his book.

In a review of Suzuki's book, considered by many to be a classic, sinologist Paul Demiéville says: "Virtually all of this country's [Japan's] culture … is interpreted in relation to Zen which has become a master key providing access to both the aesthetic (painting, poetry) and Japanese militarism." Among the "Zen arts," Suzuki attaches great importance to archery. In 1953, in his preface to another questionable classic, *Zen in the Art of Archery* by Eugen Herrigel, Suzuki praises "this marvellous little book by a German philosopher," probably unaware of Herrigel's earlier sympathies for Nazism. Whatever the case, in a strange reversal of trends, Japanese culture as a whole has now become the expression of a kind of metaphysical principle known as Zen.

Suzuki's views have also made a big impression on Japan and notably on his friend, the philosopher Nishida Kitarō, founder of the so-called Kyoto school. In his book written before the war, *The Question of Japanese Culture*, Nishida defines the essence of the Japanese spirit as a desire to become one with all things, to reach a point where there is no Self and no Other. This merging into non-duality corresponds to what Nishida calls the "pure experience" and, he claims, naturally leads on to a sacrificing of the self to serve the emperor and the Japanese empire.

"Zen is the religion of the Samurai"

The idea that Zen is the religion of warriors, known as the *bushidō* (way of the *bushi* or samurai) has been commonly accepted in the West since the days of Suzuki. It is claimed that this is simply a description of the historical reality, yet this warrants a closer look.

In this case too, the gap between theory and practice is substantial: at the time when treatises on the Way of the *bushi* or samurai were being compiled, in the eighteenth century, the days of going into battle were long gone. The Tokugawa regime coming to power in 1600 signaled the start of a long period of peace in Japan, in stark contrast to the previous era, and there were very few occasions for battle. All theories about the samurai having no fear of death due to their pure Zen spirit are just that – theories. These poor and inactive warriors became simple employees – members of the leisure class even – and had to make do with simply displaying their weapons until the new Meiji government came to power and disarmed them, tired of their idleness. The notion of Zen as a martial ideology – as advocated by Suzuki and his supporters – returned with a vengeance in imperialist Japan.

A similar tradition developed in China whereby Bodhidharma, the semi-legendary founder of Chan (Zen), was also deemed to be the founder of the martial arts tradition known as Shaolin boxing (*shōrinji kenpō* in Japanese). The name is taken from the Shaolin monastery on Mount Song in China, not too far from the Chinese capital of Luoyang, where the Indian monk is said to have lived during the sixth century. In actual fact, this tradition postdates Bodhidharma's time by several centuries and therefore has no sound basis.

A number of these clichés relating to Zen and the martial arts still prevail today. Martial arts and compassion are not necessarily incompatible, we are told, as the invincibility martial arts are supposed to bring, according to Bruno Etienne and Raphaël Liogier, "makes life a peaceful battle, an internal battle where all activities become arts of peace including, in particular, the martial arts" (*Etre bouddhiste en France aujourd'hui*). This is a purely spiritual and angelic perception of the martial arts for those who rarely have cause to fight. On an actual battlefield, things are somewhat different and a lot less noble.

Similarly, it is an exaggeration to claim that Zen and the martial arts are intrinsically linked and that, from the thirteenth century, *bushidō* became a means of practicing Zen. While the shoguns (military leaders) of medieval Japan may effectively have been followers of Zen, ordinary soldiers (*bushi*) tended rather to follow Pure Land Buddhism. The Buddha Amida promised to welcome followers into his Western Pure Land. It could therefore be claimed that Amidism seemed more concrete than an elitist form of Zen which, in teaching its followers to ignore death, seemed to avoid the serious issue of the afterlife. However, this does not seem to have been entirely the case. In practice – and somewhat paradoxically – medieval Zen became a kind of "funerary Buddhism" to such an extent that its success undoubtedly owes less to its declarations on the equal nature of life and death and more to the supposed effectiveness of its funeral rituals.

Part III
Buddhism and Society

"Buddhism is a tolerant religion"

[The] spirit of tolerance and compassion has been one of the most highly regarded ideals of the Buddhist culture and civilisation from the outset. This is why there is not one single example of persecution or of one drop of blood being shed either in the conversion of people to Buddhism or in the spread of Buddhism over its two thousand five hundred year history.

Walpola Rahula, *What the Buddha Taught*, 1959

It is often said that Buddhism is a tolerant religion, if not *the* religion of tolerance. There is no fundamental dogma or ultimate ecclesiastical authority in Buddhism. This makes it at first glance difficult to talk about orthodoxy or Buddhist "fundamentalism." However, in practice the situation has not always been as harmonious as the theory would have us believe. There have been several clashes over doctrine, for example. In Chinese and Japanese Buddhism of the eighth to thirteenth centuries CE, there was a marked trend towards adopting one single practice (for example, seated meditation or reciting the name of the buddha Amida). This practice was supposed to cover (and render unnecessary) all other practices (rituals, prayers, etc.).

Furthermore, the notion of a single principle leads to a homogenous universe where any real differences are excluded and where evil is merely an illusion, a lesser form of being. Tolerance towards the "other" (in particular towards the natives often represented by local deities) only exists where this otherness is reduced to sameness. Furthermore, while Mahāyāna may be praised for its inclusivity in texts such as the *Lotus Sutra*, this same text is striking in terms of its polemical nature and rejection of previous forms of Buddhism which are pejoratively referred to as the "Lesser Vehicle." This text is the fundamental scripture of the Japanese Nichiren sect and its lay organization, the Soka Gakkai, which are characterized by their sectarianism and forceful methods of proselytism.

However, it is the historical development of Buddhism in particular which has brought about a certain bending of Buddhist principles. The main problem resides in Buddhism's relations with the cultures it has encountered during its expansion towards the East. The attitude of Buddhists towards local religions is often cited as a classic example of tolerance. However, in reality this has often been more of an attempt to establish Buddhist supremacy: the most important local gods are converted while others are demoted to the rank of demons to be subjugated or destroyed through the appropriate rituals. Of course, this process is often depicted in Buddhist sources as a voluntary conversion on the part of local deities. The reality, however, is often somewhat different, as is indicated by various Buddhist myths which suggest that Buddhism has often sought to simply eradicate any local cults which stood in its way.

Tibet was "pacified" in this way by the Indian master Padmasambhava, who subjugated all the local "demons" (actually ancient gods) using his formidable powers. The first Buddhist king, Songsten Gampo, had already subjugated the terrestrial forces, symbolized by a demoness whose body covered all of Tibet, by "nailing" her to the ground using *stūpas* which were erected on twelve points on her body. The Jokhang monastery in Lhasa, the most sacred place in Tibetan Buddhism, is said to be the "stake" which was driven into the central section of the demon's body, her sexual organs.

A similar symbolism can be found in the myth of the subjugation of the god Maheshvara by Vajrapāni, a wrathful emanation of the cosmic buddha Vairochana. Maheshvara is one of the names of Shiva, one of the great gods of Hindu mythology. Shiva, demoted by Buddhism to the rank of demon, had committed no greater crime than to claim to be the Lord of all beings and to refuse to convert. His arrogance led to him being trampled to death – or, to use a pious euphemism, "liberated" – by

Vajrapāni. Seized by fear, the other "demons" (actually Hindu gods) submitted without a fight.

In Sri Lanka and Southeast Asia, where Theravāda Buddhism is dominant, the assimilation of local cults appears to have been less ruthless, although symbolic violence is present nonetheless. The reform implemented by the Burmese king Anawrattha in the eleventh century is typical in this regard: some local gods (*naths*) were allocated a certain role (in the form of the thirty-seven *naths* worshiped in one of the numerous temples of Pagan), yet most of them were actually thrown out of the royal city and the official religion.

Japan also features numerous accounts of indigenous gods being more or less forced to convert. Eventually a more elegant solution was found, known as the theory of "essence and manifestations" (*honji suijaku*). According to this theory, Japanese gods (*kami*) are merely "traces" (*suijaku*) or local manifestations, while their "original ground" or "essence" (*honji*) is the Indian buddhas. This meant that there was no longer any need for conversion as the *kami* were already essentially buddhas. Paradoxically, the notion of the absolute derived from Buddhist speculation enabled theorists of a new religion, the so-called "ancient" Shintō, to call the Buddhist synthesis into question. Eventually, this Shintō fundamentalism led to the "cultural revolution" of the early Meiji era (1868–73), during which Buddhism, denounced as a "foreign religion," saw a great many of its temples destroyed or confiscated. The indirect result of this was that Buddhism too began to take refuge in a purism tinged with modernity, which rejects local beliefs as "superstition."

Buddhist "Heresies"

All religious doctrine defines itself in relation to its "other." Christianity is defined by its dogma and orthodoxy and has asserted itself during the course of its history through its constant fight against heresy. Unlike Christianity, Buddhism does not strictly speak of dogma or orthodoxy; at most it speaks of "orthopraxy" or "correct practice." It could be argued that there is not one Buddhism but rather several. This plurality is due, in part, to the absence of a central authority in contrast to Christianity (and to a lesser extent Islam). It is also linked to the belief that the conventional truths of Buddhism are adapted to individual capabilities and that their value is therefore purely pragmatic, as a kind of "skillful means" (*upāya*). It is therefore rare to find a spirit of sectarianism or fanaticism in Buddhism. Japan probably comes closest to this due to the evolution of certain Buddhist schools in the medieval period. This sectarian spirit is most apparent in Nichiren and his disciples. Paradoxically, by refusing to have any ties with outsiders, followers of the Nichiren sect eventually refused to obey the shogun and found themselves banished. This type of fanatical behavior is, however, very unusual in Buddhism as a whole. Interestingly, the only other case of such intransigence in Japan relates to Japanese Christians.

Despite the lack of inquisitors, Buddhism has had its heretics at times. Traditional historians have declared certain cases in Buddhism to be "heresy," such as the case of the six "heretic masters" reduced to silence by the Buddha. In particular, there is the case of the two schismatic monks, Devadatta and Mahādeva. Devadatta, the cousin of the Buddha, has been called the Judas of Buddhist legend. His jealousy is said to have led to him dividing the community, killing an *arhat*, and injuring the Buddha – three of the five mortal sins, which resulted in him being swallowed up alive into hell. Yet his heresy was still active in India during the seventh century CE, according to the accounts of the Chinese pilgrim Xuanzang. He claims that Devadatta's primary sin was to advocate a more rigorous approach to religious practice, and in particular the strict observance of vegetarianism.

Mahādeva is renowned for his five propositions on the fallible nature of the *arhats* (in particular the possibility that they can have wet dreams), propositions which created a schism in the community. Despite the fact that this schism represents one of the stages in the formation of Mahāyāna, Mahādeva's good name was never restored, and subsequent tradition continued to accuse him of all kinds of base acts, most notably of having committed incest with his mother and killing his father before becoming a monk. His doctrine cannot, however, be deemed heretical in the literal sense of the term.

Despite the existence of various doctrines deemed to be "heterodox," the only Buddhist trend unanimously recognized as "heretical" by both its contemporaries and Japanese historians alike is the Tachikawa-ryū, allegedly founded by two Shingon priests, Ninkan (dates not known) and Monkan (1281–1357). According to its opponents, this trend preached sexual union as a supreme method of becoming a buddha "in this very body" (*sokushin jōbutsu*). This form of Tantric Buddhism was considered acceptable, although not entirely orthodox, in Indo-Tibetan Buddhism, yet provoked violent reactions in Japanese Buddhism. This boiled down to a different socio-political context rather than Japanese Buddhists being more puritan than their Indian and Tibetan counterparts. The Tachikawa-ryū was therefore banned in the fourteenth century. Despite its formal disappearance, the Tachikawa-ryū's influence continued to be felt during the Edo era at all levels of society – in the imperial palace and official schools of Buddhism as well as in the village cults.

"Buddhism teaches compassion"

Of all the values of Buddhism, compassion (*karuna*) is the one most admired by Westerners. It has even become the trademark image of Buddhism thanks to the image of the Dalai Lama as it has been promoted by the media. Unlike Christian compassion, which is restricted to humans (insofar as they are seen as potential converts), Buddhist compassion extends to all living beings. In early Buddhism, this sense of communion is based on a belief in transmigration, the law of karmic retribution that leads living beings to be reborn in various forms, both human and non-human. In Mahāyāna, it is rather because every being, even the humble earthworm, is said to possess a buddha nature. As a manifestation of that buddha nature in ourselves, compassion reflects the interpenetration of all things. It is not an ethical duty, but rather an ontological realization.

While it was already important in early Buddhism, compassion was brought to the forefront of Buddhist doctrine with the emergence of Mahāyāna during the first centuries CE, becoming a crucial element in achieving Awakening. Compassion is the ideal trait of the bodhisattvas who, unlike the Buddha, delay their own definitive entry into *nirvāna*: from the very start of a long career leading to Awakening, they vow not to leave the world of passions until they have saved all living beings – out of *com-passion* precisely – despite the fact that they know that all beings, like themselves, are in reality devoid of self and that their sufferings are illusory. This paradox of Buddhist compassion is expressed as follows in the *Diamond Sutra*: "If a bodhisattva thinks that living beings exist, he is no longer a bodhisattva."

And yet another paradox: compassion, in principle, is a passion, and the practice of Buddhism is supposed to eradicate passion of all kinds. How is it possible, then, to "suffer with" (in the etymological sense of the term "com-passion") and for other beings, which are essentially illusory, while at the same time remaining detached, "impassive"?

Buddhist compassion may also legitimize certain breaches of the rules. If the intention behind an action is taken into account, it is not good or bad in itself; an action that may appear to be bad cannot result in negative karma if the intention was good. This enables certain bodhisattvas to visit brothels so as to spread the word to the prostitutes working there. There are also courtesan bodhisattvas who bring Awakening to men through orgasm. This is the case with Guanyin, the Chinese version of the bodhisattva Avalokiteshvara, who appears as a ravishing young woman who enlightens all the men with whom she makes love. Despite its laudable motivations, this kind of behavior is likely to have been frowned upon by conservative Buddhists.

Compassionate Violence

Resorting to violence seems to contradict a Buddhist ethic based on compassion. Mahāyāna Buddhism – which is defined by its emphasis on ethics – tries to avoid this contradiction through the somewhat paradoxical notion of "compassionate murder," a splendid oxymoron. In other words, murder is permissible if it means that other beings will be saved.

Certain texts also permit murder in specific circumstances either through compassion or as a skillful means. According to certain Mahāyāna texts, a bodhisattva can kill a criminal without incurring retribution if the criminal is about to either kill others or injure a Buddhist, or if he acts through compassion for the criminal if the latter is about to create a karma for himself that will take him to hell. This position is traced back to the story in which the Buddha himself, in a past life, killed a brigand in order to save the lives of 500 traders and to avoid this brigand going to hell. In such cases, extreme violence is justified as being beneficial to the majority and an act worthy of praise given that it is also advantageous to the victim. This notion has served to justify many political executions. Contrary to the belief of various Western commentators on the subject who have dismissed this as a minority tradition – an exception which confirms the rule – in fact it seems to have been fairly widespread. Whatever the case, given our current level of knowledge it seems impossible at this stage to determine what constitutes the majority or the minority, "fundamental Buddhism" or "deviation."

The question of whether one can sacrifice one person to protect a number of people has become a familiar issue in modern society. With the threat of danger from terrorists, it has become a daily issue in relation to Israel and Iraq. The question of implementing an intermediate solution – controlling rather than killing the bandit – does not even seem to arise.

Whatever the case, this model leaves open the possibility of exceptional individuals using violence in exceptional circumstances. This represents a double standard in ethical terms, enabling one member of a group to act in a way that would be condemned in the case of others.

Theravāda doctrine sees it as impossible to kill with or through compassion. Anyone who develops compassionate intentions is no longer capable of envisaging murder, as only the evil roots of hatred and illusion can bring about the intention to kill and these roots no longer exist. In Mahāyāna Buddhism, by contrast, compassion seems to lend itself to the idea of compassionate murder. In Tantric Buddhism, monks are supposed to "free" the demons, but this is simply a euphemism for killing them. Similarly, compassion has sometimes supposedly been used during wartime to "relieve" an enemy of his wicked existence. This explanation has been applied, for example, to the action taken by the warrior-monks of medieval Japan.

It cannot be denied that the Dalai Lama's message of compassion has motivated many well-meaning men and women in both Asia and the West. The question is to what extent this message represents Buddhism as a whole or even Tibetan Buddhism, given the number of times it has been repeated and exaggerated by the media – and not always without distortion. On the other hand, we could ask to what extent it constitutes a response (appropriate yet culturally determined) to the expectations of the modern world, a world in which the American president feels obliged to talk about "compassionate conservatism" and where compassion has become an asset in electoral battles.

"Buddhism is a peaceful religion"

Where else in the world could you find a king like Ashoka, devastated at having gone to war and spending his whole life long practising contrition and penance?
Henri Michaux, *A Barbarian in Asia*, 1933

If the world had been spared the violent intrusions of the fanatic armies of Islam, it is likely that they [i.e. the two religions, Christianity and Buddhism] could have shared the world in peace.
Alfred Foucher, *The Life of the Buddha*, 1949

In an age when the Western world is finding itself increasingly confronted with the possibility of new "holy wars," Buddhism seems to offer a reassuring example of a peaceful religion. Compassion and non-violence are frequently cited as two of the principal features of Buddhism. The term "non-violence" is a common translation of the Sanskrit term *ahiṃsā*, and is usually defined as abstinence from injuring or killing others. The notion is included in the doctrines of the Buddha and his contemporary Mahāvīra, founder of Jainism, and is given a theoretical basis. Having become a fundamental moral principle in India, the notion of non-violence achieved international renown thanks to Gandhi, who applied a very broad interpretation to the term with the aim of eradicating all thoughts of hatred or bad faith. In Hinduism, this principle is linked to the notion that the self or *ātman* is never destroyed and instead transmigrates from one life to another. In essence it is thought to be identical to Brahman, the principle of all things. In Jainism, *ahiṃsā* becomes an absolute and its appliance requires considerable expenditure of energy.

93

In Buddhism, interpretations of this notion are more moderate than in Jainism. In a slightly different form, the notion has also inspired rules prohibiting the killing of living beings in the Vinaya. This abstention must be voluntary – it is the intention which matters. Within this context, murder is essentially what presents an obstacle to meditation and Awakening. Compassion, while mentioned, only plays a secondary role.

The reasons which justify *ahimsā* becoming a basic moral principle include the idea that the universe constitutes a whole and that, by injuring another person, one injures oneself; or the idea that violence towards others is morally polluting; or the golden rule of not doing to others something you would not want them doing to you.

All of these reasons are invoked at one point or another in Buddhist morality, yet the essential issue is the notion of retribution for one's actions. The law of karma means that violence nurtures violence. As a result, this moral becomes an awareness of karmic causality. On the one hand, violence is one of the general characteristics of existence; on the other, it is something which must be avoided in order to leave behind the cycle of existence for good and achieve Awakening or *nirvāna*. All forms of violence, however necessary to maintaining order in society, simply contribute to the ongoing cycle of births and deaths.

In principle, Buddhism condemns all forms of murder. According to the *Abhidharmakosha shāstra* for example: "As all soldiers are working towards the same goal, all are as guilty as the one among them who kills. In fact ... all are mutually inciting one another – if not in voice, then because they have come together to kill ... Even if forced into joining the army, they are guilty unless they make the following resolution: even to save my life, I will not kill a living being."

In the monastic discipline (the Vinaya), the murder of another human being results in expulsion from the monastic community (*pārājika*) – and is ranked in third place behind debauchery and theft and before lying. Mahāyāna Buddhism places it in first place.

The *Brahmā Net Sutra* (*Fanwang jing*), an apocryphal text that represents a Mahāyāna and Chinese adaptation of the Indian Vinaya, commands Buddhists to reject any involvement in war. The text states that each of the following six types of murder are forbidden: killing with one's own hand, giving the order for someone to be killed, killing using various methods, praising murder, watching and rejoicing when someone is killed, and killing through magical incantations.

In reality, Buddhism has a complex relationship with war, and reasons for bending the principle of non-violence have never been wanting. In countries where Buddhism represented the official ideology, it has often been obliged to support the war effort. Violence was justified by considerations of a practical nature: when the Buddhist Law (Dharma) is threatened, it is necessary to ruthlessly fight the forces of evil. Kill them all, and the Buddha will recognize his own. Murder in this case is piously qualified as "liberation," since the demons will be released from their ignorance and can then be reborn under better auspices.

Buddhism also resorts to symbolic violence in its rituals. To a modern eye this may not look like true, physical violence, but in premodern societies it was seen as very real, and was indeed often real in its psychological effects. Tantric Buddhism in particular includes a significant range of magical techniques designed to overpower demons. It has always tended to liken its enemies to hoards of demons and has sought to defeat them through ritual. The crucial moment in Tibetan ritual dances comes when the priest stabs an effigy personifying the demon forces. This ritual is thought to reenact a monk's killing of the evil king Lang Darma (803–42), a persecutor of Buddhism. Political leaders have also performed Buddhist rituals for the purpose of crushing their enemies. The Japanese emperor Go-Daigo (1288–1339), for example, sought to defeat the shogun (military ruler) by carrying out Buddhist rituals which essentially boiled down to black magic.

There were also all kinds of theoretical justifications for murder, including the idea that it is just to kill out of charity or compassion, to prevent another person from committing evil. Indeed, how can one kill at all, when, according to Mahāyāna orthodoxy, everything is empty? The person who kills with full knowledge of the facts kills no one, since he has realized that all is but illusion, himself as well as the other person. The idea, moreover, is not exclusive to Buddhism, since it can be found in a classic Hindu scripture, the *Bhagavad Gita*. A Chinese Zen text similarly states that if a murderous act is perfectly spontaneous it is of the same order as a natural disaster, and thus entails no responsibility. One also finds this sort of sophism in the writing of Zen apostles like D. T. Suzuki. Here as elsewhere, the recourse to higher truths provides justification for the worst aberrations.

In "Le Bouddhisme et la guerre" (1957), Paul Demiéville notes that, in Japan, "The religion became feudal at the same time as the society itself; armed conflicts between the sects and the imperial court, between sects and overlords, between sects and sects, went hand in hand with feudal battles." From the eleventh century, the large monasteries gained almost complete autonomy. Ordinations, which were previously controlled by the state as in China, became the privilege of some of the great monasteries. However, the majority of their occupants were merely monks by name, having never been officially ordained. These monasteries were also important land owners, and would stop at nothing to expand their estates (*shōen*) and protect them against intrusion.

It was the age of "warrior monks" (*sōhei*), who formed bands and often ruthlessly attacked anyone who threatened their interests (whether the imperial court or neighboring monasteries). Around this time, new sects also developed (Jōdo Shinshū, and Nichiren) which were both popular and sectarian and led to the development of actual "states within the state." The abandonment of celibacy by the Shinshū monks and the setting up of a hereditary patriarchate in particular led to the emergence of religious dynasties with both secular and spiritual motivations. This insubordination of the Buddhist clergy drew to a close at the end of the feudal era, marked by the establishment of the Tokugawa military rule (1600–1868). The subsequent constraints placed on Buddhism explain in part why, following the Meiji Restoration (1868), Buddhism paradoxically appeared to be incapable of resisting militarism and was swept along with "spiritual mobilization" in support of war.

Then there is Tibet, which is often claimed to be the incarnation of Buddhist pacifism. Yet we may well question the validity of this claim, given that Buddhism has not had much of a pacifying effect on Mongolian conquerors or Japanese warriors in the past. This pacifism may be little more than a necessity turned into a virtue. Certainly it has not always been this way. The real Tibet has never been a Shangri-la. It has been involved in numerous wars and has been torn apart for centuries by infighting between the various Buddhist sects. The Gelugpa stranglehold on the Tibetan *sangha*, after the fifth Dalai Lama assumed power in the seventeenth century (with the aid of the Mongols), still did not put an end to this situation. Over the following two centuries, the Tibetan armies continued to fight various enemies (some of whom were also Buddhist): these enemies included the kingdom of Ladakh, the Dzungar Mongols, the kingdom of Bhutan, Nepal, and the British.

As for the modern-day era, it could be argued that Tibet has been somewhat forced into pacifism as it does not possess the force required to clash with its powerful neighbors. To call this pacifism an indicator of Buddhist spirituality is rather like discussing the Christian spirituality of Switzerland or the pacifism of Luxembourg. When once asked why he chose non-violence to resolve the Tibetan problem, the Dalai Lama burst out laughing, saying: "Six million Tibetans. One billion Chinese!"

But can we at least say that there are no holy wars, or at least no just wars, in Buddhism? The concept of a "just war" is fundamentally Christian and cannot be automatically applied to other religions. It is nevertheless useful to discuss some of the elements which are common to Christianity and other religions where various criteria, initially discussed within a Christian context, are then discovered elsewhere. In fact, the concept of a just war seems to occur wherever it is necessary to justify war in the face of ethics which condemn violence towards others.

This state of warfare is particularly prominent in Sri Lanka, where the Tamil Hindu minority have claimed independence, resulting in bloody confrontations with the Sinhala Buddhists since 1983. Sinhala discourse is the closest thing there is to a Buddhist apology for holy war. This is, of course, a very particular kind of fundamentalism as it is based on an ethnic group and not a sacred text. There is, however, a reference text known as the *Mahāvamsa*, a mythical-historical chronicle, which documents the magical voyages of the Buddha to Sri Lanka as well as the victorious battle of King Duttaghamani against the *damilas* (Tamils) in the name of Buddhism. The *Mahāvamsa* therefore supports the belief that the island and its government were traditionally Sinhalese and Buddhist. The term Dhammadīpa ("Island of the Dharma") notably appears in the text. From here, it took just one quick step to transform Sri Lanka into a sacred land of Buddhism which had to be defended against infidels at all costs. This fundamentalism, inspired in part by the puritanical reforms of Anagārika Dharmapāla at the start of the last century, is first and foremost a political ideology.

To summarize, and without wishing to deny that an ideal of peace and tolerance lies at the very heart of Buddhism based on numerous passages from the scriptures, there is also no shortage of other sources to suggest that violence and warfare are permitted when the Buddhist Dharma is threatened by infidels. In the *Kalachakra tantra*, for example, the infidels in question are Muslims who are threatening the existence of the mythical kingdom of Shambhala. In the thirteenth century, the Mongolian invaders and the Japanese warriors putting up resistance were all fervent Buddhists.

It is important to contrast the dream of a peaceful Buddhist tradition with this darker side. Even in these recognized cases of intolerance, however, Buddhism is only guilty of not maintaining a sufficient distance from ideological or nationalistic policies or from the social setting from which it has evolved. Overall, even given the cases noted, it has been a lot more balanced in this matter than the other major religions and ideologies.

—————— "Buddhism affirms —————— that we are all equal"

The founding act of Buddhism was the battle of one man, Siddharta, against his society, the Indian caste system society.
Bruno Étienne and Raphaël Liogier, *Etre bouddhiste en France aujourd'hui*, 1997

Buddhism is often characterized as a pathway to salvation that is open to all, as a reaction against the caste system of India. This notion has always had a strong impact: in the 1950s, for example, Dr. B. R. Ambedkar (1891–1956) used this idea as the basis for his movement to help the Untouchables of India, encouraging those outside of the caste system to convert to Buddhism en masse.

By renouncing the world, the Buddha appeared to abandon the dominant values of Indian society, which include the afore-mentioned caste system. This system is one of closed social classes which include the brahmins (or priests), *kshatriyas* (warriors), *vaishyas* (traders), and *shūdras* (artisans and peasants) in addition to the "untouchables" or outcastes. This renouncement involves a rejection of differences in social status in favor of spiritual experience. It is worth noting that this renouncement occurred within Brahmanism itself and that the ascetic experience of the Buddha is part of a more general framework. By renouncing the world, the Buddha is simply conforming to relatively widespread standards of behavior, and his break with the Indian society of the day is only relative.

99

In the spirit of equality, the Buddha is said to have opened the doors of his budding community to anyone who sincerely wished to join him in renouncing the world. He himself was born into the warrior caste (*kshatriya*) and led the way for others by renouncing his royal privileges. Among his first disciples were people from all different castes: warriors of course, starting with members of his family; brahmins, members of the priestly caste; as well as some outcastes. His patrons included many merchants as well as a famous courtesan. However, some of them were important political figures, including several petty kings of northern India. These princely origins of the Buddha were not forgotten, and tradition subsequently came to emphasize royal symbolism, transforming the Buddha into the equivalent of a universal monarch (*chakravartin*).

It is worth asking to what extent the *sangha* or Buddhist community was egalitarian. The rules governing ordination indicate that not everyone was accepted. The admission process involved a sort of exam, with the applicant having to swear that he was perfectly free and healthy in body and spirit, i.e. that he was not a slave, in debt, ill, infirm – or a hermaphrodite.

In the Vinaya tradition, the Buddha comes across as more of a conformist than a bold reformer who openly rebelled against the caste system. Of course, the early Buddhist community appears to have been relatively tolerant as regards the social origin of its members, yet the same was probably also true of other groups and renouncers within Brahmanism and Jainism. In principle, monks and nuns would leave behind their society and the caste system upon which it was based. In practice, however, social distinctions remained.

While Buddhist monasteries did serve as a means of social ascent for some monks whose intellectual or spiritual talents compensated for their low-caste background, overall the social differences that characterized the profane world were maintained within the world of the monasteries. In Japan, for example, the same alliance between the "army and the church" as in Western societies was evident. In other words, a cadet from an important family was often destined for priesthood from the outset and was easily able to reach the higher positions which remained inaccessible to other monks. This was notably the case where the imperial princes (*monzeki*) were concerned, who continued to lead a life of luxury at the monastery, pulling all the political strings.

Differences in status were perhaps even more marked among the nuns, who, in medieval Japan, were often forced into religion by their families so as to carry out ancestral rituals. Nuns from a more aristocratic background led a relatively easy life with the financial support of their families, whereas those from less wealthy backgrounds often lived in abject poverty. Even today, nuns are still treated as second-class citizens in most Asian societies, deprived of certain fundamental rights and material resources.

The question of the relationship between women and Buddhism is one of the most problematic aspects of the religion. It is said that the Buddha initially refused to admit his own maternal aunt and adoptive mother, Mahāprajāpati, to his order. This was not because he thought her to be unworthy but rather because he feared inciting malicious comment. It was only after the intervention of his disciple and much-loved cousin Ānanda, we are told, that he decided to agree to the ordination of women, but not without imposing some rather severe rules on them first (due to the alleged imperfection of women, a common theme in early Buddhist texts).

These rules were entirely in keeping with the fundamentally misogynist mindset of the day. They state that nuns are inferior and subordinate to monks under all circumstances. By depriving them of the spiritual authority which donations from lay followers would have brought, the rules trapped the nuns in a state of dependence and poverty, making them particularly vulnerable to political, economic, and social fluctuations. In most cases, restrictions on the plenary ordination of nuns mean that most nuns are not fully ordained thereby condemning them to an inferior status and precarious existence.

In theory, the Mahāyāna principle of non-duality implies equality between men and women. In reality, nuns are still inferior to monks in monastic life. However, they are beginning to demand more equality now that Asian cultures are increasingly coming into contact with modernity. Nevertheless, these attempts often run into strong resistance from the ecclesiastical authorities. Recently, for example, the media reported the case of a Thai nun who was attacked by monks for having demanded an improvement in the status of nuns.

Aside from the specific case of Buddhist nuns, the relationship between women and Buddhism is characterized by symbolic and religious violence. The exclusion of women from public life takes many forms. Buddhism has for instance long imposed all kinds of taboos upon women, both nuns and lay women alike. The strongest form of misogyny is expressed in certain Buddhist texts which describe women as perverse beings, almost demonic. In Tibet as in Japan, women were excluded from the sacred sites of Buddhism as they were perceived as being fundamentally impure and were not, for example, allowed to undertake pilgrimages to certain mountains.

Worse still: the uncleanliness of menstruation and childbirth meant that women were condemned to a special kind of hell known as the Blood Pool Hell. The Buddhist clergy offered a cure in the form of rituals carried out by priests, in return for payment of course. Buddhism is, after all, supposed to save all living creatures in its spirit of tolerance, even the lowliest of beings.

In view of this, it comes as somewhat of a surprise to learn that Buddhism, notably Tibetan Buddhism, served as a refuge in the West to those women disappointed by feminism. In fact, praising women in their status as mothers is not a sign of egalitarianism; on the contrary, it is the principal characteristic of all patriarchal religions and societies. Similarly the profusion of female deities may involve a reevaluation of the female principle, yet the latter always remains subordinate to the male principle. And what of

Zen, a tradition which, in principle, is not interested in the gender of its adepts and claims that Awakening is equally open to all? At an institutional level, things are rather different. In Japan at least, the Zen "masters" are almost always men, and women only play a subordinate role. The situation has begun to change in western Zen centers, however, where female leaders are beginning to emerge.

Furthermore, while Buddhism may seem to demonstrate a certain tolerance towards homosexuality, this is more the result of pragmatism than open-mindedness: when it came to monastic discipline, homosexuality (and more specifically pedophilia) posed less of a problem than heterosexuality among the essentially masculine (and highly misogynist) monastic community. Homosexuality has long been widespread in Japanese Buddhism, and it even came to constitute a "way" in the same way as poetry, tea ceremony, and flower-arranging: "the Way of Ephebes" (*shōdō*).

Traditional Japanese monasteries were home to a class of boys known as *chigo* who served as objects of sexual distraction. These novices were unshaven and had long plaits; they wore make-up like young girls (white powder on their faces, stylized eyebrows, and red lips). They played an important part in the monastery's artistic events and in banquets held for the nobility and the shoguns.

While this is best known as a Japanese phenomenon, the situation appears to have been similar in Chinese and Tibetan monasteries. The Tibetan monk Tashi Khedrup says of the *dob-dob* monk police force, of which he was a member: "It is true that their fights were often about favorite boys, but what else can be expected in a community of only men and boys?"

In stating that salvation is accessible to all living beings and that everyone harbors a spark of Awakening, Buddhism asserts that everyone is equal, in theory. However, cultural deviations and practices have come to greatly undermine this proposition.

"Buddhism is compatible with science"

Buddhism is the science of the mind.
Matthieu Ricard, in *The Monk and the Philosopher*, 2000

Western followers of Tibetan Buddhism never miss an opportunity to emphasize the Dalai Lama's interest in science, in particular the sciences of the mind (neurology etc.). However, it would be wrong to call Buddhism a "science of the mind" if, by "science," we mean a form of knowledge based on experimental research and a materialistic conception of nature and mankind. Buddhism in fact involves a spiritualist or idealist conception which only accords secondary importance to material causality since it stems from the domain of the relative truth. Seen from this point of view, Buddhism is certainly not opposed to science, although it does not consider science to have the final say (something which should be primarily spiritual in nature).

In their efforts to modernize, Buddhists have sought to emphasize the compatibility of Buddhism with modern-day science, discreetly failing to comment on any areas of disagreement; some have even gone so far as to claim that some of the great scientific discoveries were predicted long ago by Buddhism. Concordism of this kind is more or less knowingly deluded since it refuses to admit that the supposed Buddhist ideal – Awakening – is resolutely supra-mundane and non-secular and that Buddhism can only comprehend modernity and the values it embodies as a collapse within the material (and materialistic) sphere.

Science may well claim to be supremely effective in its attempts to decipher the laws of physics, yet Buddhists feel that science is on the wrong track when it comes to the meta-physical or spiritual world, which it can essentially only deny.

Neuroscience, for instance, claims to have made immense progress over the last few decades. New technologies have enabled them to obtain ever more precise images of the smallest recesses of the brain. The model of an infinitely complex brain, whose apparently most simple and "subjective" functions (perception etc.) are distributed over various nerve centers at different levels, would seem to support the Buddhist notion of the absence of self. Buddhist theory states, for example, that the dependent origination of the various aggregates of consciousness results in the illusory notion of the self.

The success of a book like *Zen and the Brain* by James Austin reflects our hopes of scientifically understanding some of the higher states (starting with universal compassion and kindness) which meditation is said to bring. On the other hand, Zen thought and its taste for paradox has fueled a scientific approach that seeks to go beyond the traditional impasses presented by rational thought. The popular scientific book *Gödel, Escher, Bach* by Douglas Hoftstadter, for example, draws some of its inspiration from Zen *kōans*.

From the Buddhist viewpoint, the argument revolves essentially around the serious and rational aspects of Buddhist thought. The existence of a Buddhist rationality cannot be denied, yet not all rationalities are scientific. The Buddhist rationality is anchored within a soteriological framework which renders it incompatible with scientific discourse – unless it contradicts itself, either in whole or in part.

Neuroscientists are always striving to determine the neuronal correlates of various states of consciousness in the hope of reproducing these states artificially. Very little progress has been made on this front, and we are asking virtually the same questions as at the start of the 1970s when the trend for LSD and other hallucinogenic substances seemed to make mystical experience accessible to all. Buddhist meditation does not subscribe to this approach, since Buddhism is based on the notion of the primacy of consciousness while science sees consciousness as a mere by-product (of evolution and the neurological structure of the brain).

So what are the neurobiological processes which cause consciousness or, more precisely, these *je ne sais quoi* which philosophers refer to as *qualia*, subjective and indefinable qualities that form the content of individual consciousness: the specific redness of red, the emotional content of an emotion, the intangible beauty of a face or poem – let alone the mystical experience or the supreme state called Awakening? While Awakening may indeed be deemed to have a certain intellectual content – a point which has always divided the Buddhists themselves – from the Buddhist point of view, it can never be reduced to a series of algorithmic processes of the brain and to synaptic connections between its hundreds of billions of neurons.

The problem with qualia is as follows: while the objective, "third-person" mode of existence of neurons is the object of physical, objective, and quantitative description, how can neuron interactions cause subjective, qualitative, "first-person" experiences? There is a hiatus between these two modes of existence which scientific models of the brain, despite their increasing complexity, seem incapable of filling.

Scientists remain divided over the issue of whether or not dualism exists between the brain and consciousness, although they are likely remain unconvinced by the theoretical non-dualism of Buddhism. There is, however, an apparent convergence between science and Buddhism in that both recognize that everything which constitutes the self (joys and anxieties, memories and plans, a sense of personal identity) results from a concatenation of causes and effects. However, beyond this, the elements which come into play in each case are unrelated (for example the *dharmas* or physical-psychological aggregates in the Buddhist model and nerve cells and molecules in the scientific model).

Most causal explanations of consciousness provided by neurobiology are reductionistic in that they eliminate what they claim to explain. Buddhism, which sees consciousness as a primary given, is therefore unable to accept these explanations without undermining itself.

It is clear that the Darwinian theory of the evolution of consciousness (or the brain) is not compatible with a Buddhist ontology that sees consciousness (whether one calls it buddha nature or otherwise) as eternal and transcendent, even though it may not always manifest itself to the same degree in humans. For many Buddhists, the universe as a whole is the Buddha, or in other words the Awakened consciousness that manifested itself perfectly in the "historical" Buddha and must be reactivated through Buddhist practice, having been temporarily obscured among humans.

Buddhism has long presented itself as an essentially cosmological doctrine. Although the Buddha allegedly refused to comment on the eternal or non-eternal nature of the world, his disciples were eager to fill this gap in knowledge, and cosmology became an essential element of Buddhism. The Buddhism adopted by Chinese and Japanese converts was not so much a moral or religious system as a semi-"scientific" new vision of the world.

This new vision was primarily that of Hinduism. While the Buddhist context was radically new in certain respects, a definite trend towards traditional cosmology emerged as the new religion spread. Yet Buddhism could also be defined as an attempt to go beyond the cosmos. As Paul Mus noted, Buddhist cosmology is an arrowed structure – it only exists so that we can escape from it. The world is said to be like a house on fire, a dangerous place we need to escape from as quickly as possible. The universe is a cosmic scene where man's salvation takes place. Transmigration through the six destinies and the three worlds is not a goal in itself: having occupied all positions in the hierarchy of beings since the dawn of time, the individual must finally transcend this hierarchical structure.

Supporters of Buddhist modernism are often eager to reject traditional Buddhist cosmology, which they consider to be outdated and too culturally specific, favoring instead certain intuitions that are held to be universal. However, this issue is far from clear and involves a risk of throwing the baby out with the bathwater.

Take the examples of karmic retribution and transmigration, two fundamental notions in Buddhism. They cannot be reduced to simple moral or psychological causality; they form an integral part of an entire cosmological system, that of the Ten Realms: the six lower destinies still belong to the cycle of life and death whereas the four higher destinies lead to deliverance. The very structure of karma would collapse without Buddhist cosmology. The same is true of the *bardo*, the intermediary world in Tibetan Buddhism through which the spirit must pass before being reborn. Similarly the Buddhist pantheon, composed of all orders of beings populating this cosmic structure, would be reduced to a few vague psychological or spiritual principles excluding all forms of worship and devotion. Tell that to the humble followers who spend all day prostrating themselves in front of the Jokhang temple, the most sacred site of Lhasa. This temple would have no reason for being without their worship; it would simply be an empty shell that would quickly be turned into a museum by the Chinese.

In fact, the Chinese do not perhaps present the gravest danger facing Tibetan Buddhism since they are, at least, a visible enemy; this danger instead comes from some of its own supporters who, with the very best of intentions, are relentlessly striving to modernize Tibetan Buddhism, in doing so emptying it of part of its very substance. The same is true of other forms of Buddhism. Chinese leaders are also engaged in a "modernization" of Chinese Buddhism, attempting to separate the wheat (spiritual principles) from the chaff ("superstitions," a category which embodies the ritual aspect of Buddhism), to the detriment of the living religion.

According to Matthieu Ricard in *The Monk and the Philosopher*, "Buddhist cosmology belongs to the conventional truth, a truth which was that of the moment." On the other hand, he goes on to say: "The contemporary description of the cosmos corresponds to the conception of the universe we have in our day and Buddhism accepts it as such." But let's not be misled: this apparent agreement conceals a hierarchy of values, a subtle denial of science. This amounts to saying that scientific cosmology also stems from the conventional truth just like traditional Buddhist cosmology, whereas Buddhist philosophy is actually said to express the ultimate truth. For scientific minds, even if scientific theories are only temporary, the ultimate truth is nevertheless expressed in mathematical logic. Here there is a profound and apparently impassable difference between the spiritualist viewpoint of Buddhism and the resolutely materialistic scientific stance.

While early Buddhism has sometimes been described as a-cosmological, in reality Buddhist cosmology developed very early on. Two types of cosmology can be identified – the one-world system and the multiple-world system. The first is on the whole common to Hīnayāna and Mahāyāna while the second is specific to certain Mahāyāna texts. In the first system, the single universe is centered around Mount Sumeru, a sort of cosmic pillar linking the three levels of reality: the heavenly realm, the human world, and the netherworld. The human world is said to be a flat disc that rests on four layers or "wheels" – the earth, water, wind, and space. At the summit of Mount Sumeru is the Heaven of the Thirty-Three Gods, governed by Indra, a deity originally of Vedic origin. Mount Sumeru is surrounded by five circular oceans separated by mountain ranges. Four continents are located in the outer ocean at each of the four points of the compass with ours, Jambudvīpa, located in the south. The other three continents are also populated by human beings who have a radically different lifespan and are of a different size to us.

In Mahāyāna, a multiple cosmological system has also developed parallel to this notion of a sole universe. It is rather like Pascal's famous sphere whose center is everywhere and circumference nowhere. An infinite number of worlds coexist in this universe, as infinite, we are told, as the sands of the Ganges. Some are pure while others are impure or mixed, and each is the domain of a particular buddha. The world in which we live is an impure world, located in the south like the Jambudvīpa world of the previous model. This is the "field" of the Buddha Shākyamuni. This southern location is somewhat surprising, given that this cosmos is said to be infinite and composed of 3,000 large universes, themselves composed of an infinite number of smaller universes like ours. Lifespans within each of these universes vary considerably from ten years to 80,000 years.

With this notion of an infinite cosmos and a proliferation in the number of buddhas, the temporal imagination gives way to a spatial imagination. Time seems to disappear, swallowed up into a black hole. According to this conception, Buddhist salvation has become a large-scale cosmological drama: it is no longer a question of the salvation of an individual (as in the one-universe system) but of a cosmic salvation involving an incredible amount of energy and time. The *nirvāna* of a cosmic Buddha amounts to the salvation of all living beings, as these beings are none other than the Buddha himself.

As we can see, these two types of cosmology – the unique and the multiple-universe systems – involve two different types of salvation. The first case implies a slow and laborious temporal process; in the second, the buddhas and bodhisattvas (and sometimes the followers themselves) can travel to other far-away worlds (such as the Pure Land of the Buddha Amitābha) at the speed of light. The first case implies individual *nirvāna* dominated by temporal metaphor; the second, a cosmic *nirvāna* dominated by spatial metaphor. It is the first cosmological construct with its vertical layering and center symbolism which has dominated the Buddhist imagination. This double cosmology came to coexist with the Copernican cosmology after the Western expansion in Asia.

While early Buddhism was characterized by a degree of reservation as regards cosmology, the cosmological domain was predominant in Tantric Buddhism (as in Vedic thought prior to this). To be sure, the early Buddhist "Genesis" (which is both cosmogenesis and psychogenesis) was also perceived to be a process of emanation, yet this implies a degree of degradation, of falling into the flow of existence (*samsāra*) where "everything is suffering." For all the early Buddhist talk of "returning to the source," this "return" primarily aims to dry up the flow of existence by destroying the energy that drives it – desire. Tantric Buddhism, by contrast, claims to return to the source by going *through* images and symbols beyond all images and symbols. As for Chan (Zen), it claims to "cut off" all images and thinking – and therefore all cosmological symbolism.

From the outset, there were therefore two forms of practice based on radically opposed cosmologies: in one case (that of early Buddhism) involves a "fall" into the cycle of life and death (*samsāra*), leading to a radical break between two ontological planes (truth and illusion); in the other (that of Tantric Buddhism), the passage from one to multiple is perceived as a continuous emanation or "procession." Thus, while early Buddhism presents a solution of continuity between the absolute and the relative, Tantric Buddhism presupposes the continuity of the flow of consciousness. So, rather than denying the world to discover a purely spiritual reality, as do Hīnayāna and Mahāyāna practitioners, Tantric Buddhist practitioners aim at returning to the source from which they stemmed. Rather than radically putting an end to all mental activities and all desire, Tantric Buddhism advocates a transformation (or "reversal") of mental activity through desire. Rather than rejecting the world and the body, it transforms them into mandalas, into ritual images or microcosms which provide access to the reality of the macrocosm. Despite these differences between the two soteriological structures, cosmology still plays an essential role in both cases. It would therefore be impossible to eliminate traditional cosmology in the name of modernizing Buddhism without calling into question the very content of the doctrine.

— "Buddhism is a kind of therapy" —

The teachings of Buddhism are not doctrinal in essence or less still theological; they are therapeutic.
Etienne and Liogier, *Etre Bouddhiste en France aujourd'hui,* 1997

Some have attempted to go beyond the choice of Buddhism as a philosophy or religion by emphasizing that it is first and foremost a psychosomatic therapy, a kind of yoga. This therapeutic aspect has always been an essential component of Buddhism, although not always in the way we see it today. It has often been noted that Indian Buddhism makes great use of medical metaphor, and the list of the four "noble truths" is sometimes likened to a medical diagnosis. While it is indeed possible that Buddhism was influenced by Indian medical thought, Buddhist monks have also played an important role as doctors of the body and soul, despite denying the existence of the latter.

In early Buddhism, the Buddha is sometimes referred to as the "Great Physician." When asked questions of a metaphysical nature, he responds with the metaphor of the poisoned arrow: if someone is injured by a poisoned arrow, does he go to a doctor to inquire about the nature of the poison or about the identity of the archer or does he have the arrow removed? Similarly, when faced with death, it is necessary to seek deliverance urgently, and questions about the nature of the world are simply a waste of time. Despite the Buddha's pressing call to stick to the facts, this has not prevented his disciples from developing a philosophical, metaphysical, and scholastic system.

Buddhism is indeed a form of therapy, but more in a purely medical sense than in the usual spiritual sense. It is no coincidence that one of Asia's most famous buddhas is Bhaishajyaguru, the Medicine Buddha. In traditional societies, a great many illnesses (physical as well as mental) were blamed upon the destructive action of demonic influences. Buddhism and its exorcism rituals constituted a powerful antidote, a veritable panacea. Yet despite canonical Buddhism discrediting medical practice, which was said to represent a stumbling block on the path to Awakening, various monks still specialized in this practice. Canonical metaphors which depict the Buddha as a great physician of the body and mind borrow a large part of their imagery from the medical knowledge of the day.

The psychological interpretation of Buddhist meditation constitutes a fundamental aspect of modern-day Buddhism in the West. According to this viewpoint, Buddhist doctrine and art are forms of depth psychology. Esoteric mandalas, for example, are often interpreted as universal archetypes of the Jungian type. The mantras are another important aspect of esoteric ritual that present a problem, to the extent that they are a kind of magical formula. It is hardly surprising therefore that some followers of Tibetan Buddhism deny the magical aspect of the mantra in attempt to rationalize it. Mantras thus become something "which protects the mind," not from any disaster as such, but from distraction and mental confusion. This etymological definition, however, remains practically unknown among ordinary Buddhists.

Buddhism and Magic

The world of traditional Buddhism is haunted by evil. This is especially true when it comes to illness, which is perceived as being of natural, human, or supernatural (demonic) origin, depending on the case. In this haunted world, Buddhism has essentially served as a medical technique for tackling the supernatural causes of illness – the many demons and spirits which populate the invisible world. These magical attackers are not just demons; they also include Buddhist deities who are manipulated by humans during certain rituals which vary in their degree of orthodoxy. Demon or god – sometimes this is simply a question of perspective.

Divination played a predominant role in tracking down the supernatural causes of illness or catastrophe. This involved a wide range of techniques including possession and astrology. In Tantric Buddhism in particular, demons were ritually invoked through a medium, usually a child. This kind of exorcism was said to heal various illnesses and, more generally, to avert disaster. Divination was usually the preliminary stage of exorcism. The exorcism often aimed to transfer the demon who possessed a sick person to the body of the medium; from here, the demon could then be more easily chased away.

Buddhist techniques are not, however, restricted to exorcisms and protective rituals; they often constitute rituals of aggression. In fact, the line between white magic (defensive) and black magic (offensive) is notoriously difficult to pinpoint given that, as soon as one feels threatened, preventive attack is presented as a defensive action, not as aggressive action (even though it may be perceived as such by the object of the attack).

The *Mañjushrīmūlakalpa*, a Tantric text translated into Chinese in 775, describes a ritual of subjugation used for healing. The ritual requires the production of both a mandala and statuettes of the divine bird Garuda. A mantra is then recited before the statuette and a fire ritual carried out: oblation, fumigation using burnt offerings, and animal, vegetable, or even human ingredients.

Similar kinds of subjugation rituals directed at a supposed enemy are found in Tibet. Certain rituals involve the priest invoking a protector deity. He then throws his offerings in the direction of the hostile force. This sacrificial gift is intended to symbolize the flesh and bones of his enemies and the protector deity. In other cases, for example in *cham* dances, an effigy is used to represent either the demon that will be exorcised or the enemy that needs to be defeated (often they amount to the same thing). The ritual culminates with the masked dancer, representing the Buddhist deity Mahākāla, striking the effigy to "release" the demon.

In times of war, secret rituals enabled the monks to manipulate the occult forces to bring victory to their camp. The fifth Dalai Lama resorted to such rituals to conquer the armies of the king of Tsang in 1641. On the other side, similar rituals were carried out on behalf of the king. Chinese leaders also asked Tibetan lamas to perform similar rituals until the start of the twentieth century.

In China and Japan, fire rituals (*goma*) used for exorcisms were (and still are) carried out before a triangular hearth where paper figures were burnt, representing the alleged attacker. In 1329, Emperor Go-Daigo performed a ritual himself with the aim of "quickly dispelling malicious men and dissipating acts of evil" – in other words, ridding the land of the warriors who governed the country in a de facto manner.

While some of these rituals may stem from pre-Buddhist conceptions, we cannot dismiss them as relics from another age, barely tolerated by orthodox Buddhism, or as a kind of "shamanic substratum" as other authors have done. The fact that these rituals were performed by eminent monks provides sufficient indication that the conceptions underlying them have been gradually integrated into Buddhist doctrine and ritual over the ages. There are no such things as "relics" in a religion; either a conception is integrated into the living doctrine of which it becomes an integral part or else the conception becomes obsolete and disappears. Attempting to separate "magic" from "religion," as did the French sociologist Émile Durkheim in the case of Christianity, is therefore a misguided effort, out of touch with reality.

While Buddhism may be best known in the West for its high-flying philosophical concepts and meditation techniques, historically it was its arsenal of magical formulas which made it a hit with rulers. When the Buddha was first introduced in Tibet, China, and Japan, it was essentially as a god more powerful than the local deities. Similarly the Buddha's representatives, the monks, were sought after as miracle-workers or thaumaturges.

Another important aspect of Buddhism that deserves a brief mention here are supranormal powers (*abhijñā*). Buddhist thaumaturges are endowed with six powers: (1) the power to pass through objects, to fly, to tame wild animals and to transform themselves however they wish; (2) the divine eye which enables them to see the death and rebirth of all beings; (3) the divine ear which enables them to hear all the sounds of the universe; (4) the ability to read the minds of others; (5) the memory of their own past lives as well as those of others; and above all (6) knowledge of the destruction of all defilements, in other words, the end of ignorance which marks the achieving of buddhahood.

These powers are usually considered to derive from meditation and constitute one of the essential means of converting others. However, only the knowledge of the destruction of all defilement is specifically Buddhist in that it belongs to the realms of formlessness. Buddhist cosmology distinguishes three levels: the realm of desire, the realm of subtle form, and the realm of formlessness. The first five powers still belong to the realm of form and are therefore considered to be impure states.

The attitude of early Buddhists towards these powers was nonetheless ambivalent. Although the Buddha worked miracles on various occasions, he is said to have condemned his disciple Pindola for having flaunted his powers before laypeople. Without going into detail, it is clear that the argument against the use of these powers should be viewed within its socio-historical, or more precisely its sectarian, context. Given that these powers also featured in other rival religions (Hinduism, Taoism), Buddhists came to proclaim a sixth and more superior type of power or else criticized the very notion of powers in the name of the principle of emptiness. What appears to be a form of demystification is often little more than a tactical maneuver still inscribed within the mythical discourse since the doctrine of emptiness in fact played the role of a "superpower," despite the philosophical interpretations taken at face value by various exegetes.

There is no question of denying the existence of a rationalist trend within early Buddhism for whose adherents these powers were considered illusory. While this trend influenced the Pāli canon and the Western perception of Buddhism, it was far from being representative of Buddhism as a whole. Although early Buddhist orthodoxy was divided on this issue, the development of Mahāyāna Buddhism increased ambivalence about thaumaturgy. On the one hand, the Mahāyāna conception of the buddhas and bodhisattvas as miracle-workers led to descriptions in various Mahāyāna texts, such as the *Lotus Sutra*, where the Indian taste for the supernatural often seems to verge on delirium. This was certainly the view held by the first Western scholars such as Eugène Burnouf, the translator of the sutra in question. On the other hand, the logic of emptiness tended to empty these miracles of their content, transforming them into illusions or magical tricks which initially impressed the crowds but ended up simply boring them. Unlike the false magic of the heretics, we are told that the magic of the Buddha is the true, correct magic, as the Buddha has realized that the universe as a whole is simply magic. The achievement of emptiness is therefore perceived as being the supreme "power," yet it is also the negation of all powers as it both includes and annuls them at the same time.

Stories about these supranormal powers and about the "worldly benefits" which Buddhist rituals can bring represent the two sides of the hagiographical imagination. The distinction between the afterlife and this lower world is not always as definite as it seems: certain funeral rituals, for example, aim both to ensure the deliverance of the deceased and to protect against any evil the deceased person could cause if they were to come back to earth as a ghost. Ritual formulas such as the Japanese *Namu Amidabutsu*, initially aimed at ensuring the rebirth of the deceased into the Pure Land, are also said to prevent revenge by any animals or humans killed. Monks recited the formulas to ensure a good harvest or good fishing: the formula had the double advantage of magically producing an abundant harvest or fishing yields for humans and salvation in the Pure Land for any insects or fish falling victim to this pious carnage.

It is therefore necessary to question the propensity of Buddhist exegetes and Western commentators to accept charitable explanations of magical ritual, thereby overlooking the real (or symbolic) violence taking place. Despite attempts at reform, these types of practice have always been and are likely to remain both apotropaic (magical) and soteriological in nature. Sticking to a purely soteriological interpretation, like the followers of a "pure" Buddhism, boils down to misjudging the nature of real Buddhism and its history, not to mention its future.

—— "Buddhism advocates a strict —— vegetarianism"

Buddhist vegetarianism is originally derived from the Buddha's condemnation of animal sacrifice but has perhaps also been influenced by the practices of certain Hindu and Jain renouncers. The principle of non-violence (*ahimsā*) is thus expressed in the edicts of King Ashoka, which prohibit animal sacrifice and place restrictions on the consumption of meat and the categories of animals which can be killed.

The question is often raised as to whether the Buddha himself was vegetarian. Various canonical sources insist that the Buddha never ate meat. Despite this, one widespread tradition suggests that the Buddha died from eating contaminated pork. This legend has been the subject of much debate over time, and exegetes have attempted to lessen the scandal of a meat-eating Buddha by arguing that the term translated as "pork" actually referred to a mushroom dish. In *To Cherish All Life*, Philip Kapleau, an American Zen master, argues like many before him that the "pork delicacy" which poisoned the Buddha was in fact a kind of truffle. He adds, "Laying aside scholarship, what reasonable person can believe that Chunda offered the Buddha a piece of pork when the latter came to pay him a visit?"

If the texts are anything to go by, the Buddha seems to have held fairly moderate views on the consumption of meat. His cousin, Devadatta, was stricter and proposed the adoption of five rules including a ban on eating meat and fish. The Buddha refused to enforce this rule and continued to restrict the ban to ten types of meat which were already forbidden by society at that time. Monks were permitted to eat meat, so long as they were not aware of any animal being killed especially for them. The three conditions required in order for monks to eat meat (neither seeing, hearing, nor suspecting that an animal has been killed for them) are somewhat problematic given that this ignorance is impossible to prove. Ignorance about the origins of the meat being offered could also be perceived as somewhat hypocritical. Like it or not, the consumer of the meat is equally responsible for the slaughter of the animal since the demand creates the offer. While certain Buddhist texts do recognize this point, the tradition as a whole evades the question.

However, the rules gradually become stricter: initially, it is sufficient for a monk to refrain from killing an animal himself. Later on, he becomes indirectly responsible for acts committed by others. In the end, the consumption of any meat is perceived as being incompatible with the precept that prohibits killing. It no longer lessens this contradiction for the act to be carried out by a lay intermediary.

In Mahāyāna Buddhism, the consumption of meat is perceived as more problematic than in early Buddhism. Eating meat appears to represent a blatant contradiction of the Golden Rule ("Do unto others ..."). As stated by the Chinese master Guanding: "By analogy with oneself, one cannot wish to eat others." The growing popularity of vegetarianism in Brahmanic circles may have forced Buddhists to follow suit. As the *Lankāvatāra Sutra* states: If even non-Buddhists are abstaining from eating meat, how can Buddhists continue to eat it when compassion forms the very fundamental principle of their doctrine?" Ascetic motivations may underlie the prohibition of meat and fish for monks. Vegetarianism is after all a form of renunciation, the motivations for which may have very little to do with compassion. Non-observance of a vegetarian life-style is cited as an obstacle to deliverance in the *Lankāvatāra Sutra*, and could lead to rebirth in a lower realm. It seems therefore that soteriological reasons form the principal motivation here, not compassion. The cultural and demographic context also plays a large part in the Buddhist vegetarian tradition. Compassion was not always cited as a reason for vegetarianism initially: the monks were required to abstain from eating horse and elephant meat, for example, because these animals were deemed to be royal symbols.

In China, the issue of vegetarianism was the subject of much debate among clerics and laypeople alike at the start of the sixth century CE. The Chinese are big fans of meat, especially pork. The consumption of meat has always been a class privilege and meat was perceived as a "supplement" to the usual staple – rice. At any rate, meat has never been subject to any ethical taboo there. Buddhism in China therefore goes against a deep-seated culinary tradition. Total abstinence was only required during certain ritual periods characterized by fasting and purification.

The debate came to focus on other issues (ritual, economic, gastronomic, and dietary). Vegetarianism is certainly a more complex issue than it at first appears. Vegetarian monks have inherited a long-standing Chinese tradition that associates vegetarianism with reclusion and mourning.

The Emperor Wu (464–549) of the Liang dynasty was one of the most enthusiastic champions of vegetarianism. After converting to Buddhism, he prohibited his subjects from carrying out animal sacrifices and requested that the Buddhist clergy observe a strict vegetarian diet. He drew his inspiration for these decisions from the *Mahāparinirvāna Sutra*, which condemns the consumption of meat and fish – in contrast to the Vinaya texts of the Mahāyāna and Hīnayāna schools. These imperial decrees formed the subject of fierce discussion within the monastic community. Supporters of vegetarianism emphasized the prohibition on killing and causing suffering, as well as the dietary value of vegetables and various economic factors. Despite some initial reluctance, strict vegetarianism thus became a means for the Buddhist monastic community to radically differentiate itself from the laypeople. The latter, whatever their inclinations, were supposed to eat meat on specific occasions to respect various social obligations. Eventually, however, the prohibition was extended to include them as well.

Cultural context has also played an important part in Japan – sometimes pulling in different directions. Vegetarianism was abandoned by the monk Shinran (1173–1263) and his followers as it involves a voluntary aspect which went against the abandonment of self required by total faith in the Buddha Amida. Following the Meiji Restoration (1868), the consumption of meat was permitted for all monks (as was marriage) and vegetarianism only exists there today in specific places such as the Zen monasteries.

Japanese Buddhism developed the notion that all beings, vegetables included, have a buddha nature and are therefore fundamentally identical. As stated by the monk Chinkai (1093–1152): "All sentient beings have a buddha nature and will become buddhas. How could buddhas eat one another?" Following this idea through to its logical conclusion, however, means that even vegetarianism presents a problem.

While Western Buddhists are mostly strict vegetarians, Buddhists in Asia have tended to break this rule. In doing so, they perhaps felt they were following the Buddha's example. Today, perhaps they could rather draw their inspiration from the Dalai Lama who, according to a press report, when invited to dinner with various other celebrities by the French president to celebrate the fifth anniversary of the Universal Declaration of Human Rights, was presented with a special vegetarian meal instead of the meat dish served to the others, and allegedly protested, saying: "I'm a Tibetan monk, not a vegetarian."

It should also be noted that vegetarianism has often had unexpected social effects. Some sociologists have noted that vegetarianism has contributed to the "Sanskritization" of Indian society, acting as a means of facilitating social mobility within the Indian caste system. Abstaining from eating meat, considered to be an impure food, offers a means of increasing the ritual purity of a group – in this case the Buddhist *sangha*. Thus, vegetarianism has become a means of expressing social and religious differences. From here, it is just one step to social discrimination, and this line has been crossed on occasion. In Japan, for example, the *burakumin* ("hamlet people," a euphemism used to refer to social minority groups) are often discriminated against because they carry out the impure professions relating to animal slaughter. Paradoxically, a situation has arisen where social violence has taken place here in the name of non-violence.

"Buddhism is a universalist teaching"

Mahāyāna Buddhism recognizes the existence of a buddha nature in each being. Unlike Hinduism or Shintō, which are ethnically and culturally confined religions, Buddhism claims to be universal, transcending all races and specific cultures. Despite this, as we have seen, many aspects of early Buddhism reflect its Indian origins. This is particularly the case when it comes to Buddhist cosmology or the concept of karma. Attempts have been made to purify Buddhism of these elements and to label them as subsidiary or secondary. Yet this type of purification runs the risk of emptying Buddhism of its entire substance.

Furthermore, given its close ties with the state, Buddhism has contributed in many cases to the emergence of a national consciousness. A particular case in point was the contribution made by Japanese Buddhists to resisting the Mongols (also Buddhist) during the thirteenth century. The final victory brought about by "divine winds" (*kamikaze*) invoked by Buddhist rituals led to the emergence of a national ideology in Japan which saw itself as a "divine land" (*shinkoku*). This ideology played a highly important role in the imperialist Japan of the twentieth century, fueling the country's impulsive desire for conquest across the Asian continent. During World War II, Japanese Buddhists supported the war effort without reservation, assisting imperial mysticism with their rhetoric.

With the modern rise of nationalism, Buddhism found itself facing a new trend towards fundamentalism. In India, the revival of Buddhism in the twentieth century can primarily be put down to a mass conversion on the part of the Untouchables, following a social reform by Dr. B. R. Ambedkar which provided them with the glimpse of an escape from their plight. They therefore began to reject en masse the Hinduism and its caste system which had repressed them for so many centuries. Unfortunately, their claims to sacred Buddhist sites soon began to clash with the soaring Hindu nationalism, to the extent that the situation is now degenerating into a confrontation between two forms of fundamentalism.

Traditional Buddhism became an obstacle to progress and modernization, and as such was attacked as superstition. It therefore had to adapt so as to fit within the narrow framework of the modern nation-state, most notably to respond to the challenges presented by the rapid expansion of Christianity, from which it adopted certain missionary methods. Yet it is primarily by embracing nationalism in the name of modernization that Buddhists have been driven to take part in nationalist movements; Buddhism soon saw itself taken over by political agendas of an entirely different nature which had more in common with the values of the West.

In Japan, Zen nationalism is the result of interactions between Buddhism and Western modernity. In response to the Meiji reform, the Japanese created the term "New Buddhism," a modern, cosmopolitan, humanist Buddhism from which modern Zen is derived. Zen particularism claims to be superior to Western modernity and reveals hints of universalism.

In Sri Lanka, the Sinhala Buddhists were driven to emphasize their unique identity in response to attacks by Christian missionaries and began to expurgate their doctrine of any magical and superstitious elements it contained. They adopted an ever more fundamentalist attitude, seeking to rediscover the "pure" doctrine of canonical Buddhism. At the same time, they also began to identify the history of Buddhism with that of the Sinhalese nation, and Buddhism was promoted to represent a means of protecting this nation against the colonizing forces of the West. Anagārika Dharmapāla (1864–1933) in particular encouraged the Sinhalese people to find their real identity as Buddhists and to reject outside influences.

Most of the time, Buddhist nationalism has evolved in response to Western colonialism. Buddhists have sought to promote their doctrine as something which is useful to the nation, and have asserted their native character (or at least their long-standing integration) in opposition to Christianity, which has more recently been imported from the West. Buddhist nationalism went without saying in states such as Japan and Thailand which escaped colonialism. In the colonized states, by contrast, the situation was much more complicated, and in Sri Lanka, for example, the revival of Buddhism had to await independence.

In China, the Buddhist clergy sought to gain favor with the occupying forces, in this case the Japanese who were also Buddhists. This led to their being accused of collaboration at the end of the war. The Buddhist clergy in Korea also maintained close ties with the occupying Japanese, resulting in internal divides. It was only after the war that Buddhist nationalism really reclaimed its rights.

In the case of Tibet, this nationalism is more recent in origin. Although the Tibetans had long been subject to external threats, Tibetan nationalism per se was virtually unheard of before Tibet became part of the People's Republic of China in 1951. Indeed, the rise of Tibetan nationalism was due more to the charismatic personality of the Dalai Lama than to the influence of Buddhism. Despite internal disagreements, the Dalai Lama continues to form a focal point for all nationalist aspirations both within Tibet itself and in the diaspora.

As we have seen, differences between the various situations and the blurred nature of the concept of nation in some Asian countries explain the ambivalence and multiplicity of Buddhist nationalism. In the case of Japanese Buddhists, for example, the nation identified with the state, and nationalism involved unconditional support of the country in its war efforts. Sinhalese and Korean Buddhists, by contrast, distinguished between the nation and the state. Yet in certain cases, collaboration between Buddhists and the colonial powers has meant that Buddhists were not always aware of the problems posed by imperialist war and military occupation and the barrage of social injustices they bring.

In Thailand, monks are perceived (and perceive themselves) as symbols of patriotism and members of a community which goes beyond the *sangha*, or Buddhist community, to include the nation as a whole. As such, they feel compelled to participate in patriotic discourse and to justify acts of violence committed in the name of the nation.

It is evident that the Buddhist *sangha* has had to modify its doctrine when adapting to societies such as those of China or Japan. Yet Buddhist monks have often gone one or several steps further in this direction, as is evident from the participation of Japanese warrior-monks in feudal battles or the patriotic passions of the Thai and Sinhalese monks. When the Mongols attempted to invade Japan during the second half of the thirteenth century, Buddhist priests lent their support to both sides of the conflict. One of the most recent cases of Buddhist involvement was the supporting of the war effort by Japanese Buddhists during World War II. The monks often justified some of the worst forms of brutality in the name of "ruthless compassion."

Despite its universalist tendencies, Buddhism cannot be understood outside of its cultural context given that the various national

Buddhist communities are largely dependent on their respective governments and that monks and nuns claim to be citizens of nation-states and assert their patriotism. There are therefore very definite tensions between the national and transnational aspects of Buddhism. During wars which have brought two Buddhist countries into conflict (such as the Mongols of Kublai Khan and the Japanese during the thirteenth century) Buddhists have shown no hesitation in siding with their nation, despite their claims of "internationalism."

The western "rediscovery" of Buddhism during the nineteenth century led Buddhists to view themselves as participants in a transnational, pan-Asian movement, or even a universal religion. Yet these perceived affinities between all Buddhists have not prevented a national sense of belonging from taking precedence over any sense of religious belonging. It is only recently that certain Buddhists in exile, such as the Dalai Lama or Thich Naht Hanh, have been able to acquire a spiritual status which transcends their national origins. Of course, all monks are supposed to adhere to the same monastic rules, even though these rules vary slightly depending on the school and country in question. Yet adherence to the rules varies considerably. State intrusions into monastic life have also led to notable modifications of this lifestyle in some cases, thereby emphasizing national differences.

Monks and Political Activism

Buddhism is becoming increasingly engaged. This social and political involvement sometimes brings beneficial effects and sometimes adverse effects. The Protestant influence, which gave rise to what is known as "Protestant Buddhism," is particularly visible in Sri Lanka among reformist leaders such as Anagārika Dharmapāla, who emphasized the need for a "Buddhist Reform" in order to put an end to "superstitious ritualism" which he felt was responsible for the decline of "village Buddhism" or popular

Buddhism. In addition to a return to "pure" Buddhism, free from superstition and the interference of a ritualist clergy, he also called for the *sangha* to better respond to the needs of the society. Paradoxically it is this kind of involvement, intended to quash Christian criticisms of Buddhist passiveness towards social issues, which seems to be responsible for Buddhist monks becoming involved in political battles and the conflict currently tearing Sri Lanka apart. In other societies of Southeast Asia this approach has also given rise to an "engaged Buddhism" which redefines traditional goals such as *nirvāna*, in socio-political and often anti-colonial terms. For these reformers, deliverance is defined first and foremost as freedom from social, economic, and colonial oppression.

It is fundamentally the same kind of activism that is currently developing in Tibet (in revolts against the occupying Chinese), in Sri Lanka (in the fight against the Tamil separatists) and in Myanmar (in recent protests against the military junta). Despite this, local contexts are taking this activism in directions as diverse as the quest for democracy and ethnic cleansing.

Buddhism is associated with nationalism in Burma but does not constitute an aggressive nationalist force as in Sri Lanka, probably because it has never become "modern." Political activism on the part of the monks dates back to the English colonial period there, and also took place following independence and the military coup in 1962.

In September 2007, Buddhist monks marched through the streets of Yangon in prayer as a sign of defiance towards the military junta and in protest at the high cost of living. These protests soon spread to the provinces and the monks even went so far as to burn cars in the town of Pakkoku. These kinds of demonstration have been extremely rare since August 1988 when the last major confrontation took place between the monks and the regime, resulting in more than 3,000 deaths among the opponents.

The military junta which rules Burma also claims to be Buddhist. This has meant that the monks have been able to apply pressure

127

by refusing charity from the military, thereby preventing them from accumulating merits for the afterlife. The demands made by the monks were initially perceived as being strangely materialistic by the West, yet took a more "politically correct" turn when the monks rallied in support of the National League for Democracy led by Aung San Suu Kyi who was awarded the Nobel Peace Prize several years ago while under house arrest.

This case of the Burmese monks seems to differ significantly from the case of the Sinhalese monks fighting against the Tamil separatists or the Tibetan monks rising up against Chinese oppression. Yet all of these cases reflect a similar phenomenon – that of politicization resulting from the desire to reject monastic reclusion and to become actively involved in the world. This involvement is both social and political, yet this political aspect can quickly shift to become patriotic fanaticism.

Unlike the Sinhalese monks, who represent the Sinhalese majority in opposing a non-Buddhist minority, Burmese monks often come from ethnic minority groups which are mostly Buddhist. This undoubtedly explains why their involvement in protests against the military junta in 1988–90 turned to demands for democracy rather than for ethnic recognition. However, it is important not to over-idealize the situation. There are suggestions that ethnic protests are not far away. In 2003, for example, rioting broke out in which monks attacked Muslims. In general, however, Burmese monasticism does seem to have avoided the trend towards fundamentalism in asserting its identity, unlike other forms of Buddhism in Asia.

In Tibet, political dissidence spread among the monks following the invasion of 1951, and led to the Lhasa rebellion of 1959. Protests resumed in 1987, forcing the monks to make difficult choices between their loyalty to Buddhism and their monastery, on the one side, and their nationalism and loyalty to the Dalai Lama on the other. Some feel that the Dalai Lama's policy of internationalism causes Buddhism more harm than good. For them, the fate of Tibetan Buddhism – or more specifically the Buddhism of Tibet – is more important than universalist and abstract values such as human rights, democracy, or even the Tibetan nation, all of which are relatively new issues. This new militantism has required the monks to choose between respecting their Buddhist tradition and becoming involved in the nationalist fight to free Tibet from Chinese oppression.

In his memoirs, the Tibetan monk Tashi Khedrup describes a strange incident which speaks volumes about the somewhat unmethodical activism pursued by his fellow monks. A lama is arrested along with his accomplices and is accused of having made a bomb: "When the monks of Che heard of the arrests, they decided to free the lama of Reting. They acted very strangely and even went so far as to execute their abbot when he tried to intervene." This little group then set up an ambush for the soldiers: "The monks opened fire as soon as they spotted the troop but despite catching them unawares and the high number of victims among the soldiers, they did not succeed in freeing the lama." On another occasion, Thashi Khedrup describes how the Sera monastery was bombed by the Chinese. The monks, in return, produced a gun and boasted about how many soldiers they had killed. However, their fighting did not have the results they expected; monasteries were closed down and in large part destroyed by the Chinese occupying forces. This activism on the part of the monks subsequently lessened following pleas by the Dalai Lama to abstain from all armed violence. The policy of non-violence has generally been respected until the violent protests of March 2008. There is, however, a risk that it will not long outlive the current Dalai Lama.

———— "Buddhism is a religion ———— of monks"

Buddhism is essentially a form of monasticism. The *sangha* is composed of four groups: monks, nuns, laymen, and laywomen. Yet early Buddhist doctrine centers around the monastic community. The emergence of Mahāyāna has sometimes been interpreted as an attempt to allocate greater significance to lay piety. The tendency for the monks to live shut away from the world has been criticized as a reason for the decline of Buddhism during the modern era, and various reformers have campaigned for the emergence of an "engaged Buddhism." Yet history reveals that Buddhism has always been engaged and involved in political and social life – perhaps too much at times. In Indian Buddhism, alms-begging is perceived as an exchange relationship between monks and laypeople. The latter contribute to supporting the monks through their offerings, whereas the monks in return give them the gift of their teaching, the Dharma. This Buddhist "economy" remained a dominant feature of Asian Buddhism long after monasteries had secured relative economic independence as landholders.

Monasticism may well involve the pursuit of the Buddhist utopia, yet this does not mean that the monasteries are unaffected by social and political trends. The history of Buddhism is punctuated with incidences of bloody conflict between the large monasteries in Sri Lanka and Tibet and especially Japan. Violence within the *sangha* is often perceived as being a sign of the times, proof that the end is near. This is the version of events presented to us by the "story of Kaushāmbī," a prophecy of the end of Dharma which seems to be based on tales of Greek, Shaka, and Persian invasions. Following the defeat of these invaders, conflicts within the community lead to violence which in turn leads to the end of Dharma. The Buddhist king of the city of Kaushāmbī manages to defeat the enemy coalition and, to compensate for the bad karma of the battle, he invites the Buddhist monks to a big feast. Unfortunately, the different schools of monks argue, and fighting breaks out. The feast ends with the death of an *arhat*. In later versions of the story, royal reprisals lead to the end of the clergy and Buddhist law.

One reason for the decline of the Buddhist monasteries may be that the early Buddhist Vinaya provoked a reaction in Mahāyāna through its overly legalistic approach, giving rise to a more liberal interpretation based on purely moral and internal criteria such as the purity of intentions and compassion. The line between here and laxity was quickly crossed. The Tantric emphasis on non-duality, based on a reversal of values, also seemed to justify transgression from these rules of discipline.

The ethical laxity which characterizes certain Mahāyāna texts undoubtedly played a part in the outbursts of monastic violence which occurred in medieval Japan as well as in the emergence of a new category of monk known as "warrior-monks." However, Japan did not have a monopoly on these monastic militias. We know that Chinese monks from the Shaolin monastery were involved in the fight against Japanese pirates. Similarly, Korean monks played an important role from the tenth century; they defended Korea against the Jurchen, Mongol, Japanese, and Manchu invaders (all of whom were also Buddhist).

The establishment of feudalism seems to have been responsible for the monasteries turning to violence in the case of Japan. Monastic violence therefore appears to be historically determined. In the case of Tantric Buddhism, it may also be caused by deeper doctrinal or structural trends, as in the case of Indian Tantrism. From the tenth to the sixteenth centuries, Japanese monks were involved in more than 400 "incidents" – ranging from protests to pitched battles. The Emperor Shirakawa (1053–1129) is said to have named three things over which he had no control: dice, once thrown; the waters of the river Kamo when they over-flowed; and the monks of Mount Hiei. He makes reference to the way in which these monks would intervene in political disputes, sending armed bands to escort palanquins of the gods when descending upon the capital to protest against government policy. Sometimes, the very sight of these palanquins was enough to force a decision; sometimes it was necessary to resort to weapons. This tactic was initiated by the Ise Shrine and was soon adopted by all of the great centers of Buddhism (Mount Hiei, Onjōji, Kōfukuji, Tōdaiji, etc.). From the end of the eleventh century,

their attacks were no longer limited to the governmental authorities and they began to turn against one another.

The institution of warrior-monks is usually traced back to the
priest Ryōgen (912–85), who was allegedly reincarnated as a
demon to protect Mount Hiei. However, he seems to have been
very critical of the disrespectful attitude of these "monks" and
tried to implement a set of rules in order to control them. These
monks were like Japanese warriors in all ways: they rode on
horseback and carried a bow and arrow; they would cut off the
heads of their enemies and exhibit them. Their physical violence
complemented the ritual violence carried out against enemies by
the older monks.

Conflicts most frequently occurred between the monks of
Enryakuji, a large Tendai monastery on Mount Hiei and the Onjōji
(or Miidera), another Tendai monastery on the shore of Lake
Biwa, as well as Kōfukuji, one of the great monasteries in Nara.
These monasteries were partially or completely destroyed by
monks of rival factions on several occasions. When the monks of
Miidera obtained authorization to build their own ordination
platform in 1040, thereby achieving independence from Enryakuji,
the monks of Enryakuji reacted by burning Miidera down to the
ground. In 1181 they also destroyed Kiyomizu, a branch-temple
of Kōfukuji at the heart of the capital, Kyoto. As the main monasteries became large-scale land owners, their territory stretching
from one end of Japan to the other, territorial conflicts also arose
in addition to the disputes surrounding succession and doctrine.
The Tendai centre of Tōnomine, not far from Nara, constituted a
kind of enclave in this largely Kōfukuji-dominated region, and
was destroyed by the Kōfukuji monks in 1081.

All of these events seemed to confirm to contemporaries of the
day that the "final period of the Dharma" (*mappō*), was upon them.
The official date of this period had been fixed for 1052, 1,500 years
after the Buddha's presumed date of death. In this age of decline,
the monks were no longer able to live a pure life in accordance with
the regulations of the Vinaya. More specifically, since the Buddhist

Dharma and its material symbols (the monasteries and their domains) were now under threat, the warrior-monks supposed to protect them were perceived as a necessary evil.

Various Japanese historians have argued that this phenomenon is specific to medieval Japan in the sense that the armed monks and warriors represent two responses to feudalism in Japanese society. The militarization of the monasteries became inevitable as soon as they achieved the status of overlord with their extensive territories. The monks could only stick to the policy of non-violence where the protection of the monastery was guaranteed by secular powers, something which was becoming increasingly rare.

It was necessary to bring into line these large centers of Buddhism at the end of the sixteenth century in order to end to this large-scale monastic violence for good. In 1571, Oda Nobunaga (1534–82) burnt the monasteries of Mount Hiei to the ground. His successor, Toyotomi Hideyoshi (1537–98), did the same in 1585 with Negoroji, a centre of the Shingon sect, eradicating monastic militias at the same time. This bloody episode in the history of Japanese Buddhism marked the end of feudalism in Japan.

While these great monastic centers of Japan never recovered their prosperity following their severe repression at the end of the Middle Ages, the great Tibetan monasteries such as Drepung and Sera could until recently provide us with an indication of the problems, logistical and otherwise, that such a large concentration of monks can bring. On the eve of the Chinese repression in 1959, the Drepung monastery in a suburb of Lhasa was home to some 10,000 monks. At the end of the Cultural Revolution in 1976, the number of monks at Drepung had fallen to just over 300. In recent years, it has risen again to 600 or so.

Tibetan monasticism is monasticism en masse. The vast majority of the monks were placed in the monasteries as children by their parents. Even in Thailand, the monks constitute only 1 or 2 percent of the male population, whereas the figure stands at 10 to 15 percent in Tibet. Discipline must have been hard to maintain in such institutions. As in the medieval monasteries of Japan, the Tibetan monasteries had their own security service composed of monks which were known as the *dob-dob*. As has been mentioned, more is known about this group of monks thanks to the memoirs of Tashi Khedrup, which have enabled us to reassess the somewhat idealized image often associated with the monasteries. Let's take a brief look at his life. Tashi Khedrup was sent to the monastery at a very young age by his parents. Contemplative life and study, however, were not his strongpoint. Given his lively and feisty character, he opted for a more active lifestyle and joined the *dob-dob*. He says of them: "It is true that they often fight, but what else can be expected if they are allowed to cultivate strength and daring? Tashi Khedrup was especially quick to react with his knife. During one brawl, he stabbed a monk who had attacked him. Both received a whipping as punishment. The punishment seems not to have worked, as he committed the same crime some time later, this time because an educated monk had disrespected him. The arrival of the Chinese brought more and better opportunities to show off his bravery. During uprisings in Lhasa in 1959, Tashi Khedrup went to defend the Potala, the residence of the Dalai Lama, along with 400 other monks. After the Dalai Lama took refuge in India, Tashi Khedrup was one of the monks to join him in exile. During his journey to India, he became injured and lost a leg. Yet fate smiled upon him: thanks to a British scholar he met in India by the name of Richard Snellgrove, Tashi Khedrup was able to go to Britain, where he soon married an English woman. As this case of an "ordinary" monk shows, monks are men first and foremost, and the monastic community is in fact subject to the same tensions as the rest of society, despite setting the moral bar that bit higher.

Buddhist Monasticism

The significance of the monastic community in traditional Buddhism cannot be denied. The monks have always sought to cut back on what they perceive to be the laypeople infringing on their privileges. This attitude is reflected in the protests made by the monks of Ceylon (Sri Lanka today) to the king of England, King Edward VII, in 1904: "According to the laws of the Buddha, laicism is not part of religion. The members of the *sangha* are the only living representatives of Buddhism on earth." In fact, the primacy of the monks has often been undermined throughout the history of Buddhism. The boundary between monks and laypeople is less watertight than in Christianity: a monk can quite easily renounce monasticism. In Thailand, for example, a stint in a monastery is seen as an obligatory rite of passage for all young men, albeit temporary. In Japan, monks are even permitted to marry and have an active sex life. There are also all kinds of inter-mediate statuses on the scale between ordained monks and lay-people.

Tensions between the monks and the laypeople have deter-mined from the outset the history of Indian Buddhism, which was torn between the ideals of renouncement and of active com-passion. The latter notion found its full expression in Mahāyāna. In early Buddhism, the ideal of the layman status is clearly infe-rior to that of the monks; laypeople simply hope for a better rebirth, whereas the monks strive for *nirvāna*. In the Mahāyāna school, however, the lay ideal comes to challenge that of the monks. In the *Vimalakīrti Sutra*, for instance, the layman Vimalakīti ridicules the *arhats* in the name of the compassion of the "worldly" bodhisattva, implying that these disciples of the Buddha are too attached to a deluded notion of purity.

The first Buddhist monks were characterized by their renounce-ment and lived as solitary mendicants. In principle, these monks had no fixed abode and traveled the length and breadth of India for most of the year, only meeting up in summer during the rainy season. In practice, monasteries and convents quickly sprang up in the towns and villages and some monks and nuns lived there in permanent residence. The monastic life was punctuated by ceremonies which focused on ritual confession twice a month, during the full moon and the new moon. During the ceremonies, the monks and nuns would recite a list of disciplinary regulations and confess their wrongdoings. The aim of the ceremonies was to achieve ritual affirmation of purity and the cohesion of the group. Some of the urban monasteries soon began to flourish, and religious practice became tied to routine, perhaps becoming degraded in the process through the detrimental effects of material prosperity. Unlike the urban clergy, a small minority of monks continued practicing asceticism and meditation in the solitude of the forests, and their eremitic ideal did not fit in with the compromises required by life in the large monasteries. One cause of the schism that divided the early Buddhist community was the question of whether monks should possess money. The prosperity of the Buddhist monasteries was partly the result of the generosity of King Ashoka who, as a pious and zealous sovereign, was committed to encouraging reform.

Some historians claim that the emergence of the Mahāyāna spelt success for lay aspirations. On the other hand, it also meant a decline of the values of early Buddhism, judged to be too individualistic, in favor of group cohesion and collective values. It is important not to exaggerate the opposition between monks and laypeople. The laypeople are indeed more generally concerned with accumulating merits through their actions whereas the monks are usually engaged in pursuit of salvation – yet this is not always the case. Improving karma was also one of the aims of monastic practice, and in some cases ordination was seen as a means of living an easier and more sheltered life. By contrast, deliverance was not necessarily perceived as too distant a goal for certain laypeople who were trying to emulate Vimalakīrti. Of course, in many schools, ordination remained an essential prerequisite to becoming an *arhat*, yet some schools recognized that the possibility also existed for laypeople. The possibility of transferring merits obtained through ritual or meditation soon came to deprive monks of the advantage they held in early Buddhism when no one else except the individual in question was able to modify his or her personal karma. In early Buddhism, karma remained purely individual and only those with the time and inclination to engage in intense practice, in other words the ascetic monks, could expect to progress towards deliverance. As soon as the notion developed of merits being transferred from one individual (or group) to another, anything was possible, and the dividing lines became less distinct.

Certain important laypeople of the day, in particular kings, became Buddhist models during the lifetime of the Buddha. Shākyamuni himself, by renouncing the world, not only became the Buddha but also achieved the status of universal monarch (*chakravartin* or literally "king who turns the wheel"). As such, his funeral was characterized by royal symbolism. In esoteric Buddhism, the ordination of monks subsequently modeled itself on the ritual of royal consecration, a ceremony of unction (*abhisheka*) during which the new sovereign is sprayed with waters from the four oceans, a symbol of his universal reign. Like the example of the Western imagery of the two swords, spiritual and temporal, Buddhist ideology advocates harmony between the two "Wheels of Dharma" – the Buddha and the *chakravartin* king, the Buddhist clergy and royalty. This theory reached its peak outside of India, in medieval Japan.

Criticism of monastic parasitism has sometimes given rise to anti-Buddhist repression. The most violent repression in 845 saw more than 2,000 monks and nuns defrocked and a great many temples and statues destroyed. More recently, in an entirely different political context, the Cultural Revolution had terrible consequences from which Chinese and Tibetan Buddhisms are only just beginning to recover.

The significance of the monastic community in traditional Buddhism cannot be denied. However, on the one hand, monks are permitted to marry in some cultural contexts (the same does not apply to nuns); on the other hand, the influence of a lay Buddhism that emphasizes worldly existence should not be underestimated. Nowadays, the lay version of Buddhism tends to be more prominent, especially with the abandonment of the rule of celibacy. This is the case even within communities which favor a degree of closure and existence away from the world. This development goes hand in hand with a reassessment of the inferior status allocated to women in Buddhism.

Conclusion: Buddhism or Neo-Buddhism?

After acting as a foil to Christianity until the end of the nineteenth century, Buddhism has now become a cure-all for the evils of the West. What were perceived as vices in the past are now seen to be virtues. It may be that the Western attraction to Buddhism represents a surge in the popularity of spirituality rather than a return to religion, with Buddhist spirituality offering a credible response to the anxieties of the modern world. It is this idealized and purely "spiritual" form of Buddhism which I refer to as "Neo-Buddhism" to distinguish it from the various forms of Buddhism whose tradition has been maintained, albeit with some difficulty, in Asia.

Neo-Buddhism has tended to become a sort of impersonal flavorless and odorless spirituality, a kind of Buddhism à la carte. The preoccupation with spiritual interiority is merely another form of the desire for fulfillment which characterizes the individual in contemporary society. This is somewhat of a paradox, given that the Buddhist doctrine in principle denies the very notion of the self.

It is this Neo-Buddhist modernism that the media endeavor to describe when they show us the Dalai Lama in conversation with the president of the United States, or when they report on his stance on humanitarian issues or his dialogue with religious and scientific leaders of all persuasions. This movement towards modernism is also affecting Buddhists in Asia, with virtually every temple in Japan now having its own website. It is this same "Neo-Buddhism" that "Neo-Christianity" comes up against during "religious dialogues" which sometimes lead to "Zen Masses," having little to do with either Zen or Christianity. This is what happens when you put too much water in your holy wine or tea.

It is often said that it is the ideas of Buddhism which may fill a void in the West rather than the actual culture of Buddhism. But can these ideas really be so easily separated from the Buddhist culture? Such a separation is essential if the "essence" of Buddhism is universal – which remains to be seen. However, surely the ideas of Buddhism lose their vitality when taken out of their cultural context, instead being transformed into a simple philosophy – while the practice of Buddhism becomes a kind of sport, likened to judo or aikido? If we go one step further, being a Buddhist monk means undergoing an ordination process which, at first glance, seems to relate more to Buddhist culture than to ideas. In fact, in certain Buddhist schools at least, the process involves a ritual affiliation with the spiritual lineage of the Buddha. However, this Buddhist notion of spiritual affiliation appears a long way removed from the vision of Buddhism commonly held in the West, despite being dominant in Tibet and Japan for centuries. This is why transmission from master to disciple continues to play such an important part in Buddhism, particularly in Zen, which is defined by its direct transmission from mind to mind in the form of face-to-face encounter. Through such transmission, the disciple ritually becomes a master, i.e. a buddha.

Various recent studies have shown that Asians who have recently immigrated into Europe and the United States, while emphasizing their cultural differences, tend to universalize their Buddhism, making it compatible with their Western values by focusing on its modernity, rationality, and spirituality. This voluntary acculturation seems to be motivated, in part, by a desire to succeed in the world of capitalism, and involves the abandonment of certain devotional and magical practices.

The "ethnic" Buddhism they brought with them is deemed to be too devout and ritualistic; in a word, too "Catholic" to arouse interest. The many Buddhist communities which have sprung up everywhere tend to emphasize the practice of contemplation. This reflects a preoccupation with an "authentic" Buddhism which may only ever have existed in the Western imagination. This infatuation with one of the great "Oriental" religions conceals a great many "Orientalist" prejudices. The tendency to emphasize the aesthetic and "spiritual" aspects of Buddhism and to focus exclusively upon superior or internal realities prevents certain followers from appreciating the profound vitality of Buddhism and the wide range of problems it faces. A full understanding of this Buddhism and its recognition as an intellectual, religious, and spiritual resource can only be achieved through knowledge of its history and of the non-Western societies in which it developed and, in many cases, continues to prosper.

Only by adopting a critical and well-informed approach can we avoid the drift towards the Neo-Buddhism, or even "Neo-Tantrism," which seems to be conquering the minds (and bodies) of many Western followers in the wake of the New Age trend. Nowadays, Tantric initiation has been digitized thanks to the correlative powers of the internet. The metaphor of the microcosm has become a reality, and action at a distance is no longer the result of magic, or at least is no longer perceived as such. What should we make of the newly emerging forms of spirituality where the trigger is no longer the mind but rather the click of a mouse? If we stick to the notion of real presence as produced by ritual, the rampant digitization of today's world appears to bring only a semblance of presence and, as a result, is ineffective. Yet if we admit that the effect of Tantric ritual is essentially imaginary and psychological and does not involve any real communication with the invisible world, we can appreciate that the creation of the internet perhaps represents the concretization of Indra's net, the interpenetration of all things that is so important to the Mahāyāna tradition, perhaps bringing us closer to the comprehension of Tantric mystery. Everyone must make up their own mind. There are certainly a great many cases where fraudulent intention can easily be detected on the internet. One such example is the site known as Tantra.com for "a total understanding of Extatic Sex and Sacred Relationships." This is little more than a soft porn or "sexual self-help" site where visitors can purchase works such as those by author Nick Douglas – "Sexual Secrets: The Alchemy of Ecstasy" and "Spiritual Sex."

There is one point which should not be overlooked: *chakras*, mandalas, and deities are not symbols in the ordinary sense of the word. They are perceived to be more real than external reality, and followers firmly believe in them. Yet they also recognize their intrinsic emptiness. This explains the modern-day error of interpreting them "symbolically" without really believing in them and without recognizing their concrete "reality." It is essential to let oneself be "taken in" by them for their magic to work and for the rituals to be effective. Yet within a Western cultural context it is undoubtedly impossible to believe in them completely. Furthermore, in an age where "cults" and their dubious gurus are rife, abusing the credulity of disciples who are deprived of their bearings, such an approach is not without its risks. Understanding such symbolism therefore requires a sufficiently in-depth grasp of its historical and real-life context. This is the error made by the New Age movement which claims to adapt Tantrism to the modern world yet fails to take account of the underlying context of beliefs which renders Tantrism effective.

This is not meant as a rejection of all forms of Neo-Buddhism. However, the question remains as to why this spirituality still claims to represent Buddhism when it is perhaps instead a relatively moderate form of New Age spirituality. On the other hand, what reason is there to refuse the title of Buddhist to anyone who claims to represent Buddhism? Given that I have no authority to do so, I shall content myself with simply asking the question.

Glossary

abhijñā   Sanskrit term meaning "penetration," which designates the supranormal powers obtained through meditation.

achintya   Sanskrit term meaning "inconceivable," which designates awakening or ultimate reality.

ahimsā   Sanskrit term, usually translated as "non-violence," which designates abstaining from causing any harm to other beings.

Amida   See **Amitābha**

Āmitābha (in Chinese **Omituo**, in Japanese **Amida**)   Buddha of the Western Pure Land, the main Buddhist paradise.

Ānanda   Cousin and favorite disciple of the "historical" Buddha, whose teachings he memorized.

an-ātman   Sanskrit term meaning "the absence of self," or "no-self," a fundamental Buddhist concept denoting the rejection of the ego (*ātman*) as illusory.

arhat (in Chinese *luohan*, in Japanese *rakan*)   Follower of Buddhism who has reached the ultimate phase of practice; the term designates in particular the close disciples of the Buddha.

asuras In Hinduism, mythological beings who are the enemies of the ***devas*** (gods); in Buddhism, one of the six possible destinies after death.

ātman The self. In Hinduism, the divine spark that will eventually fuse with the Absolute or **Brahman**. In Buddhism, the illusory individuality.

Avalokiteshvara (in Chinese **Guanyin**, in Japanese **Kannon**) **Bodhisattva** of compassion.

Awakening (in Sanksrit *bodhi*; in Japanese **satori**, term also translated as **Enlightenment**) The supreme experience in Buddhism, and most notably in Chan or Zen. See also **Buddha**.

bardo Tibetan term designating the intermediary world between death and rebirth.

bodhi See **Awakening**

Bodhidharma Semi-legendary founder of Chan (or Zen). A native of India, he is said to have come to China at the beginning of the sixth century.

bodhisattva Literally "being [*sattva*] bound for Awakening" or "Awakened being." The term designates the practitioner who, out of compassion, has vowed to save all beings before entering **Nirvāna**.

Bön Popular religion of Tibet, strongly influenced by Buddhism.

Brahmā One of the three major gods of Hinduism, creator of the world.

brahman (in Sanskrit *brāhmana*) Term related to the previous one, designates a priest in Indian religion. The religion of the brahmans, or Brahmanism (also called Vedism) is the archaic form of Hinduism.

Brahman Designates in Vedic religion (Hinduism) the absolute, the essence of all things.

Brahmanism See **Brahman**

Buddha ("awakened") This term designates one who has understood ultimate reality, and more particularly the "historical" Buddha, Shākyamuni.

bushidō In Japanese, the Way of the Warriors (*bushi*, or samurai).

caste system According to Hindu scriptures,Indian society has traditionally been divided into four castes (varnas) – the Brahmins (priests), the Kshatriyas (warriors), the Vaishyas (traders), and the Shūdras (peasants and artisans).

Chan (in Japanese **Zen**, in Korean **Son**, in Vietnamese **Thien**) Buddhist school traced back to the Indian monk Bodhidharma. See also **Zen**

Confucianism Religious and moral doctrine based on the teaching of Confucius (Kongfuzi, 551–479 BCE).

conventional truth See **Two Truths**

Dalai Lama Spiritual leader of Tibetan Buddhism, said to be an incarnation of the **bodhisattva** Avalokiteshvara.

deva Celestial being of Hindu mythology. In Buddhism, *devas* remain subject to the law of karmic causality, and the path of the *devas* is one of the six paths through which beings transmigrate.

dharānī Incantation, often synonymous with mantra.

dharma In Hinduism, the term designates cosmic, social, and religious order. In Buddhism, *Dharma* means the Buddhist Law, both cosmic order and the doctrine of the Buddha; *dharmas* also designate phenomena or things, the constitutive elements of reality.

dhyāna Sanskrit term usually translated as meditation.

Diamond Vehicle (Vajrayāna) See **Tantrism**

Dōgen (1200–53) Japanese Zen master, founder of the Sōtō school.

dukha Pain, suffering. One of the Four Noble Truths.

Eightfold Path The way to end all suffering. It consists of: right view, right intention, right speech, right action, right livelihood, right effort, right mindfulness, and right concentration.

Four Noble Truths The four truths realized by the Buddha when he reached Awakening, namely: suffering (*dukha*), the origin of suffering (*samudaya*), the cessation of suffering (*nirodha*) that leads to *nirvāna*, and the path (*mārga*) to end all suffering – the **Eightfold Path**.

Gautama   One of the names of the "historical" Buddha.

Gelugpa   Also known as the Yellow Hat School – one of the major schools of Tibetan Buddhism, founded by Tsongkhapa (1357–1419).

Great Vehicle   See **Mahāyāna**

Hīnayāna ("Lesser Vehicle")   Term used pejoratively by the followers of the **Mahāyāna** (Great Vehicle) to designate the more conservative rival school (see also **Theravāda**).

Hinduism   Main religion of India. Hinduism (or Brahmanism) emerged during the first millennium BCE from Vedism or Brahmanism, a religion based on sacred texts called the Vedas.

honji suijaku   Japanese expression meaning "original ground" or essence and "manifested traces," meaning that the Japanese gods (*kami*) are manifestations of Indian buddhas.

Jainism   Indian religion close to Buddhism, allegedly founded in the sixth century BCE by Mahāvīra, an advocate of "nonviolence" (*ahimsā*).

Jātakas   Past lives of the Buddha Shākyamuni.

Jizō (in Sanskrit **Kshitigarbha**, in Chinese **Dizang**)   A **bodhisattva** who became very popular in Chinese and Japanese Buddhism, in particular as a protector of children.

Jōdo   Japanese term meaning "Pure Land," i.e. the Western paradise of the Buddha Amitābha (Amida in Japanese). It is also the name of the Japanese Buddhist school centered on that Buddha.

kami   Japanese gods.

karma (*karman*)   Under its neutral form, the term designates in Hinduism any act, and in particular the efficient ritual act. The retribution for acts, which constitutes karma proper, leads to a succession of deaths and rebirths called transmigration (*samsāra*).

Karmapa school   One of the schools of Tibetan Buddhism.

karuna   Sanskrit term meaning "compassion."

kōan ("case" in Japanese)   One of the riddles which Zen masters ask their disciples to solve.

Kūkai (d. 835)   Founder of the Japanese school of Shingon.

Lama   Dignitary in Tibetan Buddhism. The most important one is the Dalai Lama.

Lesser Vehicle   See **Hīnayāna**

Mādhyamika   School of the "Middle Way," founded by Nāgārjuna, circa third century CE.

Mahāsānghika   (Sanskrit: the "Great Assembly"). One of the early Buddhist schools said to have appeared as a result of a controversy over monastic discipline.

Mahāyāna ("Great Vehicle")   One of the three "Vehicles" (*yāna*) or teachings of Buddhism – the other two being Hīnayāna and Vajrayāna.

Maitreya (in Chinese **Mile**, in Japanese **Miroku**)   The future Buddha.

mandala (Sanskrit: "circle")   Circular or square diagram used in Tantric or esoteric Buddhist ritual.

mantra   Incantation or magic formula used mainly in Tantric or esoteric Buddhism.

Māra   The Buddhist Devil, also identified with Death.

mudrā (Sanskrit: "Seal")   Symbolic hand gesture used in Tantric or esoteric Buddhism.

nenbutsu (in Chinese *nianfo*)   Commemoration or invocation of the Buddha **Amitābha**.

Nichiren (1222–82)   Founder of the Japanese Nichiren school, centred on the Buddha Shākyamuni and on the *Lotus Sutra*.

nikāya (Sanskrit: "school")   The terme Nikāya Buddhism has been recently used by scholars instead of Hīnayāna Buddhism, which is judged to be derogatory. Needless to say, the latter is used here without any derogatory intention, because it is found in Buddhist texts.

nirvāna   Term by definition impossible to define, and therefore to translate; designates the ultimate goal of Buddhism, the extinction of desire, the end of transmigration from one existence to another.

Nyingmapa school   The oldest school of Tibetan Buddhism.

pārājika   Sanskrit term designating an offence or transgression that leads to exclusion from the Buddhist community.

prajñā   Sanskrit term denoting the higher wisdom, the unified consciousness.

prajñāpāramitā   Sanskrit term, usually translated as "Perfection of Wisdom."

Pure Land   Paradise of the Buddha **Amitābha**.

purusha   Sanskrit term meaning "man" or "person" – a synonym of the "self" (*ātman*) denied by Buddhism.

retribution for the acts   See **karma**

samādhi ("concentration")   Sanskrit term denoting the spiritual state obtained through meditation.

samsāra   Sanskrit term designating transmigration, the cycle of deaths and rebirths conditioned by karma. The deliverance from *samsāra* is the *nirvāna*.

sangha   The Buddhist community, which consists of four groups: male and female clerics, and lay adepts of both sexes.

Shākyamuni   "Sage of the Shākya," one of the names of the Buddha, referring to the clan from which he issued.

Shingon   School of Japanese esoteric Buddhism founded by Kūkai; its doctrine rests on the use of mantras or "true words."

Shinshū or **Jōdo Shinshū** (Japanese: "True Pure Land School")   School founded by Shinran (1173–1263).

Shintō   Literally "Way of the *kami*," or Japanese gods.

Shivaism   Religious trend of Hinduism, centred on the god Shiva.

Six Paths   The six realms of rebirth (as a being in hell, as an animal, as a hungry ghost, as a human being, as an *asura* or Titan, and as a *deva*).

Six Perfections or **Six Pāramitā**   In Mahāyāna Buddhism these are generosity (*dana*), morality (*shīla*), forbearance (*kshānti*), energy (*vīrya*), concentration (*dhyāna*), and wisdom (*prajñā*).

skandha (Sanskrit: "aggregates")   The five psycho-physical components of beings.

skillful means   See *upāya*

Soka Gakkai   Form of lay Buddhism issuing from the Japanese Nichiren sect.

stūpa   Funerary monument in Buddhism.

sutras   Canonic scriptures of Buddhism.

Tantra   Canonic text of the Diamond Vehicle or Vajrayāna; the religion based on it is also called, for that reason, "Tantric Buddhism."

Tantrism   Religious trend in Hinduism and Buddhism, based on the study of the tantras.

Taoism   Chinese religion traced back to the legendary Laozi, based on the Dao (Tao) or ultimate principle. As a constituted religion, it appears in the second century CE.

Ten Realms   This terms designates the ten realms of rebirth (the Six Paths of *samsāra* and the four higher paths leading to buddhahood).

Theravāda ("Way of the Elders")   Doctrine of the Buddhist texts in Pāli; it spread in Sri Lanka and in Southeast Asia.

transmigration   This term usually means the passage of the soul from one body into another. In Buddhism, however, its meaning is somewhat different inasmuch as there is no soul that transmigrates, but only a series of existences linked together by **karma**. See also *Samsāra*

trishna (Sanskrit: "thirst")   Term designating the craving that is the cause of existence and suffering.

Two Truths   Mahāyāna Buddhism distinguishes conventional truth, according to which things exist, and ultimate truth, according to which everything is empty. The perception of these Two Truths as complementary constitutes the Middle Way.

ultimate truth   See **Two Truths**

upāya Skillful means or expedients used to guide beings toward awakening.

Vairocana (in Japanese **Dainichi**) Cosmic Buddha; he is particularly important in the Japanese Shingon school.

vijñāna Sanskrit term meaning "consciousness."

Vinaya Discipline. Monastic code of Buddhism.

Vishnu One of the three main gods of Hinduism, he appears under various forms or avatars.

Vishnuism Religious trend of Hinduism, centered on the worship of the god Vishnu.

yin and yang The two main categories of Chinese thought, representing the female and male principles, respectively.

zazen Seated meditation.

Zen Japanese form of **Chan** Buddhism. Introduced in Japan in the ninth century, it became one of the main schools of Japanese Buddhism in the thirteenth century.